W9-AFB-253

A

Keep Your Nurses

& HealthCare Professionals

for Life!™

4 Imperatives to Inspire, Retain,
Motivate and Empower Patient Focused Nurses
(& Everyone Else!)

BRIAN LEE CSP

Mastery Publishing
Calgary, Alberta
www.keepyournursesforlife.com

C

$29.95 Soft Cover
First Edition 2001 by Brian Lee CSP

Lee, Brian
Keep Your Nurses & HealthCare Professionals for Life: To provide an implementable blueprint for leadership to significantly improve staff retention.
ISBN 0-921328-07-9
1. Customer Service   2. Business Improvement
3. Hospital/Healthcare

© 2001 Brian Lee, Custom Learning Systems
ISBN 0-921328-07-9

Publisher: Mastery Publishing Co.
                 #200, 2133 Kensington Road NW
                 Calgary, Alberta T2N 3R8
                 Phone: (403) 245-2428
                 Fax: (403) 228-6776
                 Toll Free: 1-800-66-SPEAK
                 Email: info@customlearning.com
                 Website: www.keepyournursesforlife.com

Printed and bound in Canada
Copyright 2001

To provide healthcare leadership with an implementable blueprint to significantly improve nurse retention.

- ❏ Brian Lee CSP is one of North America's leading experts in the field of Healthcare Patient Satisfaction and Change Leadership and is author of "Satisfaction Guaranteed . . . How to Master the 6 Secrets of World Class Customer Satisfaction."

- ❏ For two consecutive years, the International Customer Service Association Conference has evaluated Brian as the number one rated Customer Service Speaker in the World.

- ❏ Healthcares' Mr. "Customer Satisfaction" travels over 150,000 miles a year, delivering over 120 keynotes and seminars, and has spoken in 58 states and provinces and 12 countries worldwide.

- ❏ As both a speaker and implementation consultant to over 100 Healthcare Organizations and Fortune 500 corporations, Brian is sought after as an advisor/coach to senior management, specializing in long term strategic solutions.

- ❏ He has been awarded the National Speakers Association Professional Designation CSP (Certified Speaking Professional), becoming one of less than 20 in Canada, and less than 500 in the world.

- ❏ Brian Lee founded Custom Learning Systems Group Ltd. (CLS) in 1984. Headquartered in Calgary, Alberta, CLS has offices in Winnipeg and Toronto, and serve it's client roster of 6,000 organization with a team of 32 world class trainers and communication professionals.

Put Brian Lee to work for your next conference or meeting.

1–800–66–SPEAK (667–7325)

• Keynotes • Seminars • Consulting • Coaching

(for information, see Customer Responsiveness/Professional Development page 213)

I DEDICATE THIS BOOK TO
NURSES EVERYWHERE
WHO MAKE A PROFOUND
DIFFERENCE IN OUR HEARTS,
OUR HEALTH AND IN OUR LIVES
EACH AND EVERY DAY.

Acknowledgements:

The following individuals are gratefully acknowledged for their contribution, encouragement and support:

PAT MCFARLAND,
The Association of California Nurse Leaders

DEBBIE ELICKSEN

VALERIE CADE-LEE

GAIL CADE

JENNIFER JENSEN

SUE KRAWCHUK

JOHN SIMMONS

ROBERT LEE

Keep Your Nurses

& HealthCare Professionals

for Life! ™

*4 Imperatives to Inspire,
Retain, Motivate and Empower
Patient Focused Nurses
(& Everyone Else!)*

Keep Your Nurses

& HealthCare Professionals

for Life!™

4 Imperatives to Inspire,
Retain, Motivate and Empower
Patient Focused Nurses
(& Everyone Else!)

Table of Contents

Table of Contents

Foreword

Job #1 is to keep the good people
we've already got."
Brian Lee CSP

"We were once thought to have the best care
in the world but it can't stay that way
unless we're willing to make changes."
Canadian-raised, Dr. Martin
Shapiro, UCLA Faculty of Medicine

Imagine ten years from now. You're riding your bike through a
scenic city park, skillfully meandering in and out of pedestrian
traffic and you come towards a steep gravel decline. As you
descend, your wheel catches the corner of a large rock, causing
your bike to spin out of control. Sliding sideways, your bike
falls out of your grasp, leaving you lying bruised, battered and
bloody while pedestrians watch in horror. Shaken and light-
headed, you pick yourself up and notice a significant gouge in
your left arm that obviously needs stitches. Someone offers to
take you to the hospital but it's the weekend. The waiting room
is thick with dozens of patients and there is no room to sit
down. You wait and wait. Twelve hours pass and you're still

waiting. The lineup of patients has not depleted, in fact, it's increased. The unit clerks are visibly stressed and snap at everyone who comes in. There is only one nurse on duty. She is in her fifties and her face wears a permanent scowl. Doctors can be heard barking orders but there's nobody there to answer them so they have to take blood, fill nebulizers and attach electrocardiograms themselves.

Unrealistic? The healthcare sector in North America is facing its potentially greatest challenge in a century. For every one nurse entering the healthcare profession, four are leaving. And its going to get much worse before it gets better.

Why? Just for Starters:

Too few nurses for too many patients, mandatory overtime policies requiring nurses to work through physical exhaustion, early release of un-recovered patients in view of needed beds or because insurance companies won't pay for longer stays are all facts of today's hospital environment. While these are just a few of the contributing factors, most nurses will tell you the main reason people are leaving the profession in droves is that they feel devalued and unappreciated.

A recent poll of 1,000 of the largest companies in North America by Robert Half Corporation showed that lack of recognition and praise is the number one reason employees leave an organization.

This exodus will soon reach epidemic proportions.

One of the healthcare industry's biggest enemies is its culture and rooted behaviors. Unless leadership and staff make a concentrated effort to change their culture and transform their environment, they are doomed to repeat the past. Band-Aid treatments, "Flavor of the Month" training incentives and policy disclaimers do not work.

Our goal in *Keep Your Nurses & HealthCare Professionals For Life* is to focus on an immediately implementable leadership strategy that works. A process that will create a quality of life so supportive in the current workplace that nurses would never think of leaving or working anywhere else.

It can happen. But after reading this book, what you might do is take this information, stick it in your in-basket to be dealt with at some future date. Then you'll forget about it. When you think about it again you'll feel guilty. Guilt leads to depression and depression leads to suicide and as you know, there is already a nurse shortage. I want you to finish this book and create your own game plan. I guarantee you'll find the contents invaluable.

> *"Difficulties exist to be surmounted."*
> **Ralph Waldo Emerson**

A quick bit of history: In 1995 - 1996 my training company, Custom Learning Systems Group Ltd. achieved a dramatic breakthrough for increasing patient satisfaction scores at St. Mary Medical Center in Long Beach, California.

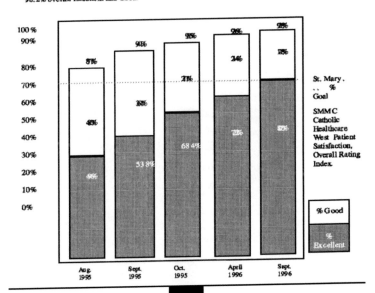

"St. Mary Medical Center (Long Beach California) Increased its "Excellent" Rating of overall Customer Satisfaction by 21.5% in less than 120 days", and continues to improve it to a remarkable 98.2% overall Excellent and Good.

Overall Patient Satisfaction skyrocketed from 46% excellence to 80% excellence in less than 18 months.

We named the process **"The Service Excellence Initiative."**

Since then we've been discovered by one hospital after the other. Because of our success, I decided to devote our training practice to healthcare – especially hospitals.

The evolution began with teaching customer service to front line staff. Based on previous experience we realized that we were wasting our time unless we inspired management to treat their front line differently.

One manager asked me, "If I give you my staff to train for half a day, what guarantee can you give that they're going to change their behavior?" I replied, "If I train your staff for half a day, what guarantee will you give me that you will lead and inspire them effectively in the other 364 days, to reinforce what I teach them?"

It became evident to me that to successfully train the front line we had to first provide leadership training, especially empowerment. It had also became evident that the organization's culture had to change. We discovered that to affect meaningful culture change, the front line – the people who actually do the work – had to play a leadership role. The way I like to say it is "For culture change to work just fine, it must be led from the top **and** the front line."

While our efforts were primarily focused on world class patient satisfaction, we noticed an interesting by-product. Greg Harrison, Director of Business Development, Central Region at Sutter Medical Center in Sacramento, California, reported to us that in two years of implementing Service Excellence, staff turnover went down 11 percent. That translated into at least a $1 million dollar a year saving for a hospital of 5000+ employees and volunteers.

As a nursing crisis stares the industry in the face, it's occurred to us that we ought to be sharing this knowledge. We then took the next step... to develop a seminar focused on nurse retention, and the book is based on our live seminar "Keep Your Nurses & HealthCare Professionals for Life."

Think of this book as an implementable blueprint for nurse retention. We've created four key imperatives to inspire, retain, motivate, and empower patient-focused nurses and everybody else. In the following chapters, you will learn how to:

1. Implement these cultural imperatives so those nurses will never want to leave.

2. Unlock the genius of nurse empowerment through front line ownership and accountability.

3. Significantly enhance employee morale and patient/customer satisfaction at the same time.

4. Create powerful incentives to improve productivity.

5. Stimulate your existing staff to become enthusiastic sales people for new recruits.

6. Involve physicians in improving nurses' quality of work life through teamwork, and reducing needless stress and conflict.

There are four key imperatives of the "K.E.E.P." strategy in "K.E.E.P." Your Nurses for Life:

K = The Key is Culture

E = Empowerment is the Way

E = Education and Engagement

P = Physician Acceptance

The Key is Culture: Culture is an organization's way of life. Programs don't work. Campaigns don't work. We've all been through the flavor of the month and flavor of the year. If you have a staff retention issue, it's likely your culture has a lot to do with it.

Retention will be won or lost, department by department, unit by unit, charge nurse leadership group by charge nurse leadership group. How else can you explain two adjacent departments, one with a great culture and low turnover, the other with a crummy culture and high turnover? I'm going to provide you with a guideline on how to create a preferred culture.

Empowerment is the Way: Another expression I like to use is: "Give your people the gift of adulthood." Until your front line owns your problems, you'll never solve them. The process of getting financially lean has preoccupied healthcare leadership for the past decade. We've stripped almost all meaningful decision making from intelligent front line people who desperately want to be able to use their own wisdom and good judgement. You will be provided with the tools to empower your staff.

Education and Engagement: "When your people are learning, they're not leaving." When front line staff is engaged; they're not enraged. How do we empower staff so they're part of the process and not part of the problem? How do we make them our chief recruiters instead of allowing them to get ready to leave? Give your people a cause that captivates their imagination and stirs their soul. Let the provision of quality patient care become their primary focus. You will learn how your front line can become your best recruiters, teachers and role models.

Physician Acceptance: I believe Healthcare's dirty little secret is the way too many doctors treat nurses. There are exceptions but it's a sad commentary that so little literature is addressing this critical problem. We achieved significant insights in this area within the past year. I'm going to share with you a model, complete with "how-to" action steps.

Finally, I want to share with you the Keep Your Nurses & HealthCare Professionals for Life "D.O. I.T." Action Plan, (D.O. I.T....stands for *Daily Ongoing Implementation Tactics*) a step by step action blueprint to assist you to realize the goals you set for yourself as a result of this input.

To be clear, let me clarify the topics I will not be covering in this book.

I will not spend time on

1. **Legislative Lobbying**

   While building political support for increased funding and healthcare reform is critical, national nursing plus state and provincial healthcare organizations are aggressively pursuing the necessary changes.

   I have, however, provided an addendum of nursing associations in the belief that all members of this proud professional should actively support their local voice.

2. **Criticizing Government or Managed Care**

   While many believe government policy and managed care are the root causes of the problem, I respectfully refer these concerns to the democratic political process and #1 above.

3. **Public Relations/Professional Image**

   While the image of healthcare and the nursing profession has suffered considerably during the past decade, and while there was a massive need to re-educate the public about the noble mission of this occupation, this is clearly a long term problem in need of long term solutions. I believe that every nurse has to become an advocate by speaking in the community and to schools to present a better image of the profession. This book is dedicated to an action process that can make a difference now.

4. **Student Career Orientation**

   Nursing leadership clearly recognizes the need to speak directly to junior and senior high school students and to encourage them to consider nursing as a career.

   While the initiative can produce results in 3-5 years, I shall defer this strategy to local hospitals and healthcare associations.

5. **Recruitment Strategies**

When it come to sophisticated recruitment strategies including the use of the Internet, there are literally hundreds of cool ideas around available from recruitment experts. I encourage you to get educated about leading edge, best practices and use them. As for the book, our focus is to assist readers to create a culture that new recruits (and old timers) will never want to leave.

We also believe that the most powerful marketing tool you have are enthusiastic, loyal employees who recruit their former classmates, peers and friends to come to work along side them.

By the conclusion of this book I hope you share my belief that by inspiring, retaining, motivating, and empowering patient-focused nurses and everybody else, your organization and your patients will benefit substantially. After all, isn't that why you chose to work in this field?

Brian Lee CSP

THE

"BIG PICTURE"

IN

STAFF RETENTION

Chapter One

FOCUS ON WHAT'S
REALLY IMPORTANT

"Satisfied needs do not motivate.
It's only the unsatisfied need that motivates.
Next to physical survival,
the greatest need of a human being
is psychological survival –
to be understood, to be affirmed,
to be appreciated."

Stephen Covey
The 7 Habits of Highly
Successful People

To look is one thing.
To see what you look at is another.
To understand what you see is a third.
To learn from what you understand
is still something else.
To act on what you learn is all that
really matters.

Anonymous

Every once in a while a profound insight into life arrives unsolicited in my email inbox, like this conversation the writer listened into on his radio one day.

"Tom and John were having a conversation and John said something about "a thousand marbles." I was intrigued, so I stopped to listen to what he had to say.

"Well, Tom, it sure sounds like you're busy with your job. I'm sure they pay you well but it's a shame you have to be away from your home and your family so much. It's hard to believe a young fellow should have to work sixty or seventy hours a week to make ends meet. Too bad you missed your daughter's dance recital."

John continued, "Let me tell you something, Tom. Something that has helped me to keep a good perspective on my own priorities." And that's when he began to explain his theory of a "thousand marbles."

"You see, I sat down one day and did a little arithmetic. The average person lives about 75 years. Now, I multiplied 75 times 52 and I came up with 3,900, which is the number of Saturdays the average person has in their entire lifetime.

"Now, stick with me, Tom. I'm getting to the important part. It took me until I was 55 years old to think about all this in any detail," John continued. "By that time I had lived through over 2,800 Saturdays. I got to thinking that if I lived to be 75, I only had about 1,000 of them left to enjoy.

"So I went to a toy store and bought every single marble they had. I ended up having to visit three toy stores to round up 1,000 marbles. I took them home and put them inside a large, clear plastic container, right here in the sack, next to my gear. Every Saturday since then, I have taken one marble out and thrown it away. I found by watching the marbles diminish, I could focus more on the really important things in life."

When it comes to healthcare there are so many really important things to focus on: patient safety, financial solvency, bio-technology convergence, joint commission accreditation, aging facilities, physician issues, unfriendly news media and patient information privacy.

Yes, these are all really important, but of what consequences are they if there aren't sufficient nurses to care for the patient.

If only it were just nurses. A dozen other healthcare occupations from Pharmacists to Radiology Technologists are in diminishing supply.

Time is running out. The average nurse's age is between 42 and 48, which means most of them will retire soon. But who will replace them? U.S. nursing school enrollments have dropped 20.9 percent from 1995 to 1998 (Source: Harvard Nursing Research Institute). The proportion of nurses under the age of 30 has dropped from 30 percent to 12 percent. Significantly fewer women are choosing nursing for a career. According to the U.S. Department of Health and Human Services, 1,754,000 nurses will be needed in the United States by 2020 but based on current trends, only 635,000 will be available.

We know that one of the reasons young people do not become nurses is because healthcare is perceived as a less-than-desir-able work environment. We hear horror stories in the news almost every day. To the gen Xer's we now depend on as a pool of new recruits, this is almost a nightmare. Why has nursing become such an unappealing profession?

1. New nursing recruits are slower at picking up the workload and physicians lack tolerance towards them.

2. In so many communities housing is expensive.

3. While older nurses like twelve-hour shifts/three days a week/it can be physically hard to work.

4. Learning the new technology of healthcare today is a constant challenge. People are afraid of things they don't know.

5. Nurses like to work in specialty nursing but it's impossible for many hospitals to afford to have a dedicated unit. There is a dilution of specialty nursing as a result.

6. Floating and cancellation of staff is frustrating.

7. There is a group consensus that money spent on recruitment outweighs money spent on retention.

8. There is virtually no one available to train new employees.

9. There are many attractive career alternatives to nursing. Many women are now choosing to become doctors instead.

10. There are restrictions that come with unionization.

11. It's difficult to entice recruits to remote locations.

12. Unacceptably low state-mandated minimum staffing ratios have had a negative impact on workload and quality of care.

13. Nurses are worried that the level of care has become unsafe.

14. Physicians are perceived to be disrespectful.

15. The volume of workload is overwhelming and many nurses don't want to work that hard.

16. Nurses are physically and mentally fatigued or tired.

17. Many hospital departments have unrealistic expectations about what nurses can or should do.

18. Patient/family expectations are increasing.

19. Nurses believe they spend more time on paperwork than patient care.

20. Mandatory overtime is physically and mentally draining and it many, in fact, endanger patient care. Working back-to-back 12-hour shifts is not uncommon.

21. Nurses are required to supervise unlicensed staff.

22. Hospital-based nurses, not only work every other weekend, but are too often, not getting time off for breaks or vacations.

23. Nurses perceive the hospital scheduling processes to be unfair.

Is it any wonder nursing has become known as "the reluctant profession"?

Staff want to feel valued and appreciated. They want to be understood, affirmed and appreciated. Look at your own personal relationships. How important is it for you to feel appreciated and valued? Nurses take their most productive hours of the week and devote them to a public institution, how would that differ?

Nurse leaders need to create an environment where people actually want to come to work because they're made to feel like they really do make a difference.

There's a story about an alcoholic patient who made frequent trips to the Emergency ward. The staff grew increasingly frustrated with him because he wouldn't take care of himself. They were sometimes less than polite. He later died of exposure and through his obituary, the staff learned about his remarkable life before the bottle. He had served in Europe during World War II and before that, he was a star pitcher for a National League baseball team. He hid from his demons and disappeared into the bottle after the war. He likely didn't set out to be an alcoholic just as healthcare professionals didn't enter the field to become distant or cold-hearted service providers.

Why do most nurses go into nursing? To make a difference in the lives of their patients. In order to inspire staff, we need to give them a cause. What better cause than World Class Patient Care/Customer Satisfaction? We all need to remind nurses that the ideals and beliefs that motivated them to enter the profession are more important than ever. If today's administrators and nursing leadership can re-ignite those beliefs, then anything is possible

We need to get better at systems and operations. We need to improve clinical outcomes, focus on customer service and we need to get the agenda back centered on people issues. We need to embrace change.

To make these changes, we have to do two things. Like the corporate world, whether it's for profit or non-profit healthcare, we must continue to reduce costs and improve our outcomes simultaneously. Therein lies the challenge. Like any other industry, people always want more value for less cost.

Chapter Two

THE TRENDS IN
HEALTHCARE

*"Unfortunately people-issues have
dropped off the agenda in favor of cost-cutting.
Most administrators, are in a survival mode,
trying to keep the doors open."*
Brian Lee CSP

We have to reestablish the Agenda. Regrettably, what you've already read about nursing challenges is a common denominator to nearly every healthcare institution in both the United States and Canada. The following trends reflect today's environment.

1. Nurses do not believe their salaries and wages are keeping pace in today's economy.

2. There is a strong public anti-tax attitude.

3. The Internet is playing a key role by arming patients with a wealth of information. In fact, the number four reason people use the Internet is for healthcare information.

4. Advanced surgical techniques and new drug therapies are expensive.

5. There is widespread opposition to increases in taxes and healthcare premiums at every level.

6. Administrators are cutting the one area that gives them immediate bottom line results—staffing levels.

7. It's a fact that, in the next fifteen years, nearly half of registered nurses will be of retirement age. With nursing school enrollments down, the time is now to attract new recruits.

8. The largest segment of the population, baby boomers, will also retire in fifteen years. At the same time, they will increase the demand for healthcare services.

9. Cost cutting and the focus on financial bottom lines outweighs the focus on patient care and quality health.

10. A growing market emphasis on customer satisfaction has increased patient frustration with the system. Long lineups and waiting lists are all too common.

11. The industry is in denial over responsibility for its role in nursing shortages.

12. The message was sent to training facilities that fewer nurses were needed due to increases in technology and prior layoffs.

13. Cost-cutting measures have sent an increasing number of patients to access hospitals only through Emergency wards.

14. Errors leading to patient deaths have increased dramatically.

15. Inner city hospitals are closing to make room for new facilities in more affluent communities, providing substandard care to specific populations.

16. The medical profession is blinded by custom and refuses to accept other treatments such as chiropractic and naturopathic solutions in conjunction with traditional medicines.

In the healthcare system, measures to help increase market shares through mergers and acquisitions has enabled a smaller number of conglomerates to control a broad concentration of healthcare resources.

In the United States, the Balanced Budget Act of 1997 has taken billions of dollars out of healthcare, and in Canada, Federal and Provincial Government cutbacks have squeezed the system to the breaking point.

A trend affecting the general workplace environment also plays a role in the healthcare industry. Institutional environments aren't all that attractive to the Generation Xers (people in their 20's and early 30's). Younger workers prefer to choose independent contract work that is less stressful so they can opt for more personal time. Even money can't make them choose between a professional and personal life. However, teamwork and strong management are much more appealing than bureaucratic institutions.

Chapter Three

THE FACTS AND ISSUES IN NURSING TODAY

*The greatest discovery of my generation
is that a man can alter his life simply by
altering his attitude of the mind.*

William James

To fully appreciate the impending crisis, we need to take a closer look at 10 interesting facts.

1. **Demand for Nurses Grows**

   Jobs for RNs will grow 23 percent between 1999 and 2006 — faster than the average for other occupations. Source: U.S. Bureau of Labor Statistics.

2. **635,000 Potential Shortage**

   The future: 1,754,000 nurses will be needed in the U.S. by 2020 but only 635,000 will be available based on current trends. Source: U.S. Department of Health and Human Services. (This equals a 1.1 million shortage).

3. Everyone is Getting Older

The aging work force: The average age of nurses is 42 to 48 and those nurses will retire soon. The proportion of nurses under 30 has dropped from 30 to 12 percent and significantly fewer women are choosing nursing as a career. By 2010, 40% of nurses will be 50 years old or older.

4. Half the Work Force is getting Ready to Leave

Barely more than half (51%) of healthcare workers surveyed this year by Aon Consulting and the American Society for Healthcare Human Resources Administration, intend to remain with their current employers for several years.

5. Half the Nurses will be Retiring

In the next 15 years, nearly half the registered nurses in the country will be of retirement age.

6. Nursing Enrollments are Down

U.S. nursing school enrollments dropped by 20.9 percent form 1995 to 1998. Source: Harvard Nursing Research Institute. Fall of 19% - down 4.6% in every region plus a 1.9% decrease in master's degree programs.

7. Baby Boomers aren't Babies Anymore

Baby boomers, our largest population cohort, will retire within 15 years and dramatically increase their demand for healthcare services. The impact: Their demand will coincide with the exodus of retiring nurses, creating a deficit in supply to meet baby boomer needs and expectations.

8. Signing Bonuses are a Way of Life

U.S. hospitals are paying up to $5000 signing bonuses and $3000 in relocation expenses.

9. The Cost of Housing is a Problem

Valley Hospital is having a tough time finding employees who can afford to live in the notoriously expensive Colorado resort town, Aspen—where the average price of a home hovers around $3.5 million and the monthly rent on a studio apartment is as high as $2000.00 (Modern Healthcare). The hospital board voted Nov. 13 to pay $4.8 million for a 31-room ski lodge that will be turned into employee housing (Modern Healthcare).

10. **Hire Nurses the E-Bay Way**

Hospitals pinched by a shortage of registered nurses may soon locate them and buy their services routinely in cyberspace. That's the hope of a company launching a web-based marketplace that allows hospitals to bid for nurses' services.

I recently spoke at the California Healthcare Association Rural Healthcare Symposium and it's expected that by the year 2020, California will be short of at least 60,000 nurses. There are about 500 hospitals in the state. If you take that 60,000 and divide that by 500, that equals a shortage of 120 nurses per hospital. That's how critical this issue is. What that also means is that rural hospitals won't have any nurses. Time is running out.

CANADA-AT-A-GLANCE

1. **Aging Nursing Population**
   - From 1993 to 1998 there was an increase of 19% in the number of Canadian nurses over 50 years of age, while simultaneously there was a 32% decrease in the number of nurses under 29 years of age. (Canadian Institute for Health Information)

2. **Flight of Canadian Nurses to US**
   - There are more than 3270 Ontario nurses in the US, including 870 in Texas.
   - Nurses surveyed left for lack of jobs (68.2%), family issues (27.5%), pay and benefits (23.1%), travel and weather (18.9%) and cost of living (4.1%). (The Canadian Press)

- One Calgary nurse is passionate about Canada, but she says it can't compete with lower taxes, higher pay and more interesting cultural opportunities. When she was last in the US she was making $22 US an hour, but the shortage of nurses has become so acute, the travel nursing company she was working for is now upping the ante to $33 US per hour. And friends of her in California say they can get as much as $70 US an hour if they are called in for an extra shift.

- A survey suggests most of the 3720 Ontario-trained nurses living abroad are interested in coming home – provided they're guaranteed full-time jobs. (The Canadian Press)

3. **Declining Nurse Populations While Population Increases**

- From 1994 to 2000, the number of registered nurses per 10 000 people in the Canada declined from 80.3 to 75.4, a decrease of 6.1% (Canadian Institute for Health Information)

4. **Increasing Costs of Finding Nurses**

- The Calgary Health Region has hired an international recruitment firm to scour the world for new staff. Recruiters are targeting the US for Canadian nurses who want to return.

- It wants to hire another 300 nurses by March, 2002 – It's willing to pay up to $8000 in relocation expenses for recruits living outside Canada and $3000 for new employees moving from other parts of the country.

5. **Impending Critical Shortage of Nurses**

- A University of Toronto study released in June, 2001, estimates that 14,000 of Ontario's 81,000 registered nurses will retire by 2004, a staggering 17.3%. This figure does not take into account the possibility of early retirement by nurses. (Canadian Press)

Chapter Four

WHY ARE NURSES LEAVING?

"The human spirit is stronger than anything that can happen to it."
George C. Scott

There is a growing perception that the nursing profession isn't much of a profession. New recruits aren't signing up and professionals are leaving for 10 main reasons:

1. **Compensation.** Thanks to the cutback era, the perception is that this is not a well-paid profession.
2. **An aging workplace.** With the average age in the mid-forties, retirement is just around the corner.
3. **Working conditions.** Nurses and beds were expendable during the recent cutback era. Current staff levels

are dangerously low, restricting time with patients and emphasizing emergency rather than preventative care. Bed shortages have led to long waiting lists, forcing the sick to line the hallways with gurneys. This creates short tempers, frustration and increased stress on nurses.

4. **Generation Xer Values.** New recruits are difficult to come by, as younger employees prefer time over money. They want an active personal life and to have autonomy over their positions. They desire collaborative leadership.

5. **Non-healthcare options.** Political science, engineering, law, finance, social work, business management, non-profit organizations and entrepreneurship...there are a multitude of choices outside the healthcare industry. Most of these positions provide what Generation Xers (prime recruits) are looking for...a balanced professional and personal life and control over their futures.

There was a time when nursing was one of the few limited professions being offered to women. Not long ago women experienced a "glass ceiling" that discouraged them from aspiring to positions such as doctors, lawyers, business managers and financiers. Now women can be whatever they choose. Nursing and medicine has always been home to remarkable individuals who have championed excellence. Among those who pushed for change in the medical profession in North America were:

Sara Josephine Baker: She was the first American woman named to an administrative or executive position with the Department of Health. Her travels through poor immigrant housing and watching babies die at alarming rates led her to instill the idea of preventative medicine.

Clara Barton: Her profession was teaching but the Civil War led her to nurse wounded soldiers. She later founded the American Red Cross in 1881.

Elizabeth Blackwell: Blackwell entered the Geneva School in 1948 after being denied access to eleven medical schools. She was refused work at every American hospital in 1949 so she traveled overseas to study, then returned to New York to open her own practice, becoming the first American woman doctor. Her New York Infirmary for Women and Children was the first American hospital to employ an all-woman staff.

Emily Howard Stowe: She met with closed doors to Canadian all-male medical schools and was forced to head south to learn at the New York Medical College for Women. After graduation in 1867, she returned to Toronto to become the first woman to practice medicine in Canada. Stowe founded the Toronto Women's Literacy Club in 1876 and coordinated the Women's Medical College in Toronto in 1883.

Ann Augusta Stowe-Gullen: Emily Howard Stowe's daughter achieved what her mother couldn't. She was the first woman to receive a medical degree in Canada.

Adelaide Hoodless: A lobbyist for domestic and civil sanitation and the prevention of disease, she established a domestic science that would influence change in the handling of food and basic cleanliness. The Victorian Order of Nurses, national YMCA and the National Council of Women were created as a result of her founding the Women's Institute.

While women still make up the majority of nursinghood, there is a percentage of male nurses who are also serving patients.

6. **A strong economy**. The world is full of opportunity. People have the choice to do whatever they want to do and get paid whatever they want to receive. Even with the recent economic slowdown, the vast majority of young professionals have multiple career choices.

7. **The profession's perceived instability**. When the public reads about the healthcare industry, they see turmoil. There are daily reports about staff shortages, disgruntled unions, liability, and early releases that cause complications leading to serious and terminal conditions. Nurses themselves have given up hope for the industry.

8. **Less education funding**. Education and training programs were cut as hospitals called for fewer nurses and budgets were lean.

9. **Computerized Medicine.** The trend towards computerized diagnostic and treatment methods tends to depersonalize patient care and put nursing into the hands of machines rather than individuals.

10. **Increased stress.** Staff shortages and long patient line-ups are forcing the issue of mandatory overtime. It's not unusual for nurses to work two 12-hour shifts back-to-back. Nurses have less opportunity for recovery time before they are called to work their next shift. They are physically and emotionally drained and see no end in sight.

11. **Lack of appreciation.** Most nurses don't receive as much as a thank you from managers or their physician colleagues. As the demands upon their time increases, nurses see very little recognition.

Every time we conduct a focus group with front line staff, over and over again, with the rare exception, nurses tell us that the message they keep hearing from physicians and management is that "they aren't very good." "We never get any positive affirmation." "They'll always tell us we've made a mistake but where's the recognition when we do an exceptional job?"

Primary "Soft" Concerns

If we analyze these ten reasons and look between the lines we can conclude there are also three primary "soft" concerns that nurses and prospective nurses don't feel are being addressed:

1. **Lack of Fairness at work**
2. **Lack of Care & Concern** from the employer
3. **Lack of Trust** in the individual

To address these "exit" issues let me make 4 key recommendations:

1. **Chief Retention Officer (C.R.O.)**

    Make nurse retention a #1 priority. You saw the figures. What's the alternative?

    Appoint a Chief Retention Officer. It should be your Chief Nurse Executive or Chief Operating Officer.

2. **Nurses Retention Officers**

    Designate every nurse leader as a "Nurse Retention Officer." It should be part of every nurse leader's job description.

3. **Appoint a Nurse Retention Project Team.**

    Ideally the team should represent all units and specialties with a 50% / 50% balance between management and front line.

4. **Ask Everyone Three Questions**

    If you read nothing further please read this. It may be the most important piece of advice I can give you:

How many times have you had a valuable employee quit and said to yourself, "If I had only known he or she was about to leave."

The following three questions will enable you to avoid the ugly surprise:

1. Ask everyone. *"If you were going to leave, what would be your number one peeve?"*

    If they reply, "I'm not leaving." Nicely ask them again (and again). Most will tell you what you need to know.

2. *"Do you reserve the right to change your mind?"*
    The answer to this question serves them notice that it's okay to change their mind and that is your intent.

3. *"What would cause you to change your mind?"*

Their answer will give you some pretty good clues about what you need to do next.

Wouldn't you like to know the answer to these questions before someone leaves? Ask everyone. This will give you the necessary insights to know where and how to begin fixing the problem.

Chapter Five

THE LINK BETWEEN EMPLOYEE MORALE AND CUSTOMER SATISFACTION

A 1% change in employee morale equals a
2% change in Patient Satisfaction
Press, Ganey

A Press, Ganey report concluded that a 1% change in employee morale equals a 2% change in customer satisfaction. Should this surprise anyone?

Until healthcare front line staff feel valued and appreciated and cared for as "internal" customers it's unlikely there will be much of a positive change in patient satisfaction. In many ways today's primary care providers are treating their customers better than they are being treated.

There is a direct connection between nurse retention and patient satisfaction. Let's acknowledge the obvious. Primary care providers want to spend more time at the bedside. They want quality contact with their patients. Remember the good old days when a nurse could afford to spend an extra five or ten minutes to give their patient a massage? I hear nurses say, "We have time to ask the patients how they are but we don't have time to listen to the answer."

Therefore today's healthcare leadership must take the necessary step to move on both fronts because they both depend on each other.

A powerful motivator to encourage administrators preoccupied with financial statements is to share the frightening economics of staff replacement.

Let's calculate the cost of turnover. I want you to think about this guideline every time you lose a nurse. Each time, it costs 150 percent of that person's annual compensation to replace them. So if you're paying a nurse $50,000 a year, it's going to cost you $75,000 to replace them. Now that doesn't include the cost of advertising, orientation, equipment costs and more. Those come from different budgets but if you add them in together with travel and time, the expense is closer to $95,000. Multiply that out by however many nurses you have lost. You will get the executives' attention by showing them this formula. It reinforces why it's so important to create a nurse retention program.

Chapter Six

EXCELLENCE

IS THE ANSWER

*"We should not let our fears hold us
back from pursuing our hopes."*
John F. Kennedy

Too many of healthcare leaders today are either overwhelmed by the complexity of clinical and operational problems plus competing and changing multiple priorities or are near burnout from the overload.

As an antidote for this malaise, I propose you consider utilizing a powerful and personal self-management tool.... it is called "Excellence."

This is a good time to define excellence. First let me say what it is not. Excellence is not doing 1 thing 1,000% better. I doubt there is one that you could do 1,000 percent better. If there is, must be either brand new or pretty awful right now.

Yet, I'll bet there are plenty of things you could do one percent better. And better and better and better.

As Jan Carlzon, the President of Scandinavian Airlines said, "Excellence is doing 1,000 things 1% better!"

Excellence is a commitment to the little things that matter to your customers.

For example, when you take your clothes to the dry cleaners, they have to have some kind of identification so your clothes don't get lost. Fair enough. But do they have to staple it to my shirt?

Why can't they put it through the buttonhole so there's less damage then I don't have to use what little fingernails I've got left to remove them? Now, is this a little thing or a big thing?

I phoned my dry cleaner once and complained. He said he would solve the problem but nothing changed. I phoned him a second time and he blamed it on the staff. I phoned him a third time and asked him to cancel my credit card account. I now only do business with dry cleaners that have taken my Satisfaction Guaranteed customer satisfaction seminar.

He didn't quite get it that this little thing made all the difference in the world to me.

Chances are it's the same with you and your customers... it's the little things that makes the big difference too.

Excellence is daily continuous improvement.

I saw a bumper sticker a few years ago that said, "The little things in life don't mean anything."

It's the little things that mean EVERYTHING!

I was visiting a friend on the West Coast and had an interesting conversation about relationships with his mother, who had been married to his father for 45 years. She told me that in the 45 years they had been married, her husband had never said, "I love you."

I found this quite shocking, so when her husband, my friend's dad, dropped into the kitchen where we had been talking, I said, "What do you mean you've never told your wife you loved her in 45 years of marriage?"

He said, "Look, on our wedding day I told her I loved her and that I'd let her know if I ever change my mind!"

Now is that a big thing or a little thing? It's a little thing that makes a HUGE difference.

I have a question for my male viewers. Have you ever noticed when you're flying on an airplane and you go to the bathroom, it is virtually impossible to keep the toilet seat up? Whenever there's a slight hint of turbulence, you've got a real mess to deal with. Wouldn't you think after decades of flying experience, the airlines could come up with something to prevent the seat from falling?

How about a hook, or Velcro, or maybe they could hire someone to hold it up! Is this little thing a big thing? Well, if you're a professional speaker about to speak to 1000 people and you've only got one suit, it could be a big thing!

It really is the little things that count.

What would be the value of improving 1% a day at your job? Let's test out this idea. Let's imagine you've completed an e-seminar and you're excited about applying what you've learned to your work. And let's say you're scheduled to work Monday to Friday next week. On Monday, if you wanted to, could you improve the way you provide service to your customers by 1%? For example, after you say thank you to your customers, invite them back and say, "Come again" or "When will I see you next time?"

On Tuesday, could you communicate with your co-workers 1% better?

On Wednesday, could you learn product knowledge about your service or product 1% better?

On Thursday, could you organize your workspace or desk 1% better?

On Friday, could you organize your time 1% better?

All right, so you've had a highly productive week, now you take the weekend off.

On Saturday, could you exercise or eat healthier 1% better?

On Sunday could you improve your relationship with your life partner or family member or friend or roommate 1% better?

Is this believable? Is this achievable? Very!

Well, do this for say, 250 days in a year, how much more valuable would you be to your employer, to your friends and family or for that matter, to the world?

This is what's so exciting about excellence!

I was speaking to my association of professional speakers and afterwards a friend came up to me and said, "Brian, I can't believe how much you've improved since I heard you last."

"I better have," I replied. "I've spoken 250 times since you heard me last."

What I love about what I do, is that every day, I learn new ideas from my clients and newspapers and magazines and from the people I meet. Every time I present, I look forward to improving my presentation by 1%. I have a question for you. Do you have one or 5 years or 10 years or 25 years of experience at what you do? Or do you have one year of experience that you've just repeated one or five, 10 or 25 times?

You see, excellence is nothing more than being the best you can be. What is the alternative to being your best? It's not being the worst you can be. I honestly don't believe that people set out to be the worst. It's being mediocre. It's being average. It's being like my former girlfriend used to describe me, "ADEQUATE." Now there's an epitaph for your gravestone. "Here lies Brian Lee. He was adequate."

It's not being like the creed for a company by the name of "Universal Widgets" "WE'RE NO WORSE THAN ANYONE ELSE." Because the issue for you and I is not how anyone else is doing, it's how well are we doing compared to how well we know we can be. Comparing yourself to anyone else can only lead to one of two outcomes. To become VAIN or BITTER. That surely is not the answer.

In our company, we are continuously improving our programs. Sometimes I think it drives the office team crazy with the continual changes but when you read this book, I hardly think you want to read yesterday's ideas.

Irving Berlin wrote a famous song for his musical "Annie Get Your Gun," "Anything you can do, I can do better."

I loved the music but not the words so I rewrote them.

Anything You Can Do, YOU Can Do Better!

"I can do whatever, just a little better. Aiming to aspire, just a little higher. Adequate is not enough. The mission for me is the best I can be."

Above all, excellence is not perfection. Perfection looks for what's wrong. Excellence looks for what's right. I really like the idea of perfection for manufacturing and products, especially when it comes to the jet motor on an airplane that I'm flying on. But when it comes to service and people, we need to let them know what they're doing right.

A perfectionist can never be done, can never be finished, and can never get anything exactly right. What I observed many years ago is, if you stay at the job long enough to get everything done exactly right, you may never go home. And if you do go home, you'll never leave your work at the office.

In this millennium, maybe we shouldn't just learn from our mistakes, maybe we need to learn from Other People's Successes. And my guess is, success may lie in doing something we haven't done before.

There's a saying, if you "Keep doing what you've been doing, you'll keep getting what you've got." The author Stephen Covey, of "The 7 habits of highly effective people," which I highly recommend, defined insanity as "doing the same thing the same way and expecting a different outcome."

The way I like to summarize and apply these ideas about excellence is:

"The secret of personal and professional excellence is to 'learn one new idea every day and do it in a better way.'"

Vince Lombardi, that great motivator and football coach, said this:

"The quality of a person's life is in direct proportion to his or her commitment to excellence, regardless of their chosen field of endeavor."

I have not found a field of endeavor, or a job, that could not benefit from this concept of excellence.

OK, so lets take a minute to summarize what we've just learned.

1. Commit to excellence to being the best you can be.
2. Excellence is NOT doing 1 thing 1,000% better. It is doing 1,000 things, 1% better.
3. Learn one new idea every day, and do it in a better way...and finally
4. The only person we really compete against is ourselves. Ask yourself at the end of each day,

"How much did I contribute to life, compared to what I know I'm capable of?"

D·A·I·L·Y E·X·C·E·L·L·E·N·C·E D·I·A·R·Y

Year	"Excellence is doing 1,000 things 1% better"		
Month	Date	#	*"Ideas, skills, improvements or systems that I learned or did today that will make me more effective in serving others tomorrow."*

Chapter Seven

Learn From
O.P.S.

BEST PRACTICES IN NURSE RETENTION

The absolute best way to solve a problem is to learn from "O.P.S."... Other People's Successes.

In researching the literature on nurse retention I discovered an excellent resource of best practices assembled by "The Nursing Executive Center" of Washington D.C. entitled "Reversing the Flight of Talent." Let's take a look at 10 Best Practices organized into three categories:

    I.   Focus on New Hires

    II. Addressing Hospital Wide Priorities

    III. Retention: At the Front Line

I. FOCUS ON NEW HIRES

Practice #1: Accelerated Specialty Orientation

Hospitals train new graduates and inexperienced nurses for specialty positions through the use of highly structured orientation program that intersperses classroom and practical learning; goal to reduce vacancy rates and minimize training costs by hiring new graduates for specialty positions and accelerating entry into staffing mix.

Practice #2: Peer Hiring Screens

Using behavioral interviewing techniques, staff nurses participate in the process of interviewing and selecting candidates for RN positions on their shifts and units; primary goal to improve new employee selection by screening candidates for compatibility with unit work environment; secondary goal to improve support for new hires by giving current staff accountability for hiring decisions.

In other words, get good at hiring right the first time. As an inexperienced manager in the past, I might ask the question, "We get pretty busy around here, how do you feel about overtime?" Of course, what is an applicant going to answer? Anything to get the job.

With behavioral interviewing, I would ask, "In the past, what has been your response to a request for overtime?" This answer will be more of an honest one and it will lend you insight into that person's character.

Use peer interviews. If you have three people on your short list of applicants, assign three or more of your staff to interview them and recommend the finalist. That includes housekeepers, interns, orderlies, everyone. Think about it. These people have to work together. If you don't involve your staff, it's possible you could make a bad hiring decision and guess what? They won't give this new employee any support. If staff help make the decision, they are much more committed to make it work. It also says to your staff, "we trust you."

In our office, this practice is standard operating procedure. When we hired our receptionist, Georgia, everybody in the office interviewed her. She felt honored that there was so much interest in her. She wanted to work for a company that took the time to really get to know her and vice versa. And yes, it turned out to be an excellent fit.

Practice #3: New Hire Support Program

As a supplement to the clinical orientation program, your hospital should schedules regular peer support groups, individual mentoring sessions, and social events for all new graduate hires; goal to improve new hire retention by enhancing support systems available to nurses.

II. ADDRESSING HOSPITAL – WIDE PRIORITIES

Practice #4: Market-Based Compensation Recalibration

Annual compensation review supplemented by targeted adjustment of pay practices throughout the year using data collected from exit interviews and variety of informal sources; goal to prevent compensation-driven departures by responding quickly to compensation changes at competing institutions.

In today's dynamic labor marketplace, you have to pay market value. I recommend a goal to pay in the fiftieth percentile of the compensation range in your market area. This allows you to make timely adjustments and prevent compensation-driven departures.

Practice #5: Compensation Fact Sheet

Human resources department regularly produces and distributes newsletter to all employees describing compensation strategy and policies; goal to prevent nurse dissatisfaction with compensation by improving nurses' understanding of the full value of their pay and benefits package.

Every nurse knows someone at another hospital that's getting paid more for the same work. That's not necessarily true but this mythology permeates the workplace and you then appear unreceptive, uncompetitive, uncaring or a combination of these. By producing a fact sheet, the figures are there in black and white. Conventional wisdom will always prevail in the absence of fact. Make it a one-page sheet by profession and include research from the market area. Also include benefits. Staff generally have no idea about the cost of benefits. You could have incredible staff ratios but if nobody believes you, what does it matter?

Practice #6: Customized Scheduling

Hospital adopts policy of customizing schedules to the needs of individual nurses whenever possible, establishes process for timely evaluation of and response to all individual scheduling change requests; goal to prevent nurse departures by accommodating specific scheduling preferences of individual nurses.

Practice #7: Structured Staff Scheduling

Unit staff create and implement a series of protocols to ensure that self-scheduling process is equitable and meets nurse, unit, and hospital needs; goal to improve satisfaction with scheduling by increasing nurse involvement in scheduling process and educating nurses about unit staffing needs.

K =

THE KEY IS CULTURE

"The philosophy, drive and spirit of an organization (culture) are even more critical than it's people or physical attributes."

Thomas Watson, Jr., CEO of IBM

Chapter Eight

CHANGE YOUR CULTURE

*"Change your culture or be doomed
to repeat the past."*
Brian Lee CSP

*"In the final analysis, change sticks only when
it becomes 'the way we do things around here',
when it seeps into the very bloodstream of the
work unit or corporate body. Until new
behaviors are rooted in social norms and
shared values, they are always subject to
degradation as soon as the pressures associated
with the change effort are removed."*
**John Kotter, Leading Change,
Harvard Press**

Culture is the "way we do things around here." It's "an organization's way of life." It's what people talk about on their coffee breaks, if they get coffee breaks. It's the rules when there are no written rules.

Whatever you decide to do after reading this book, avoid at all costs making it just a program or campaign, because when the pressure is off, your people will revert to the way it was.

As long as you call what you're eating a diet, you're implying that it's temporary. Afterwards you'll return to your former eating habits and nothing will have changed.

I want you to think about a lifestyle change as opposed to a diet. When healthcare was forced to resort to dramatic cost reduction, in many ways it attempted to take nurses out of the picture and download many related primary care duties to assistants. This was called "patient–focused care." How well did you see that work?

When a group of administrators, and or senior management sit around a boardroom table to brainstorm ideas for a new strategy, on a scale of 1-10, how good are they at creating that strategy? Yes, pretty damn good, I'm sure. The group will throw out ideas, post them on a flip chart, have someone transcribe them, have them typed and printed then give the final document an impressive name.

How much planning is initiated prior to the strategy being executed? Oh? You're going to increase the market share by 30 percent in that specialty area? How? Oh, we're just going to do it. What do we always seem to skip when it comes to executing the planning?

All right! Now that the strategy is in place, it's time to execute. So when do we let everyone know about what their role is in executing the strategy? Usually the day before.

How much do we involve front line staff in the planning? Hardly ever. What's the staff response to the strategy? Well, it's not that they don't like what you are attempting to do. It is just they did not understand the change. They F.E.A.R. what they don't know. "F.E.A.R." is an acronym for "False Evidence Appearing

Real." Change is exciting when we do it, threatening when it is done to us. You can just hear the front line staff response, "These people don't know what they're doing."

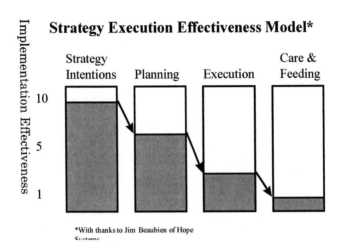

Strategy Execution Effectiveness Model*

*With thanks to Jim Beaubien of Hope Systems

Your efforts to reorient or reinvent yourself as a nurse–friendly, customer and employee driven culture is all about change.

Most organizations do a poor job of executing their change strategy. You need allies. Which means involving the people who actually do the work in strategizing and planning your new process from the very beginning.

For culture change to work just fine, it must be led from the top and the front line. As a guideline, your nurse retention project team should be a joint management front line effective (for instance, 60% / 40% or 50% / 50%).

Together is the way!

Chapter Nine

REINVENTING
CULTURE

Change is exciting when it is done by us, threatening when it is done to us.

The world does not know much about cultural change.

If you were at a bar with your front line nurses and their honesty was facilitated with the assistance of their favorite alcoholic beverage, what words would they use to describe the culture of their work unit?

Invite your nurses to describe their work environment's current culture. Remind them it's okay to put something positive on the list. In most cases the list will not be pretty. Then ask them, to brainstorm a "preferred" culture. In other words, if they could as a group, take control of their current work environment and reinvent it, what would they replace it with? Here's an example:

Current Culture	Preferred Culture
Negative	Positive
Victimized	Empowered
Fatigued	Re-energized
Stinks	Challenged
Apathy	Involved
Task Driven	Customer Driven

This is an invaluable exercise. It not only provides your team with a picture of how their workplace environment is perceived; it allows people to talk.

Awareness is half the solution. Adults, when they're treated like adults, always conclude that things can be better.

Ask them, "would our current culture sustain World Class Satisfaction for both patients and employees?" (Start off with your management team and say, "I need 15 minutes to talk to you about where we're at.") I further recommend you:

1. Conduct an assessment of your current culture and share it with everyone.
2. Utilize input from everyone to help you define your current culture and brainstorm your new preferred culture.
3. Make management accountable to institute the necessary changes "with and through" everyone else.

Remember! "50 percent of employee satisfaction comes from their relationship with their boss." (Source - "Love'em or Lose'em")

A great way to start is to write a vision statement for your team's culture. Make it an exciting description of what you aspire to become. Challenge your staff to take ownership by authorizing your vision's goals. Here are a few examples:

"A fully empowered cohesive team who feels recognized and rewarded for contributions to the organization."

"An empowered work force that feels valued."

"An energized staff that's a caring team; that's empowered to solve its own problems and feel good about it."

I received a letter from Dr. David Tillman, M.D, and current CEO of the Motion Picture Television Fund, who took the time to acknowledge how we had successfully intervened at St. Mary Medical Center to transition to a better culture. Dr. Tillman's words are testimony to the strategy that culture can change, and in fact, it's necessary that change goals are permanent and long lasting.

To wrap up this chapter, let's look at his words;

Brian Lee CSP

Custom Learning Systems Group, Ltd.

Calgary, Alberta

Dear Brian,

I am writing to thank you for the contribution that you and the Custom Learning Systems Group have made to St. Mary Medical Center. I would encourage you to use this letter as you introduce your programs to other hospitals. I am absolutely convinced that you can bring the same value to them that you have brought to St. Marys.

As you know, we identified Service Excellence as a key hospital goal during 1995. We wanted to design a program and change our culture in order to improve patient satisfaction with particular emphasis on increasing the number of patients giving us superior ratings. We wanted to involve our staff in designing and implementing this effort and we wanted it to become a part of the culture at St. Marys-not just a one time program that is quickly forgotten.

To date, we have accomplished each of our goals. With your assistance, about 55 of our staff – Service Excellence Advisors – designed and presented a 3-hour program for all of our employees. On their suggestion we have initiated several efforts including modifying our patient satisfaction survey, establishing a fund so that employees can access up to $250.00 for solving patient problems, and established a similar program for the staff from our doctors' offices. Most importantly, I believe that our employees now feel a greater sense of responsibility for keeping patients, families, and doctors satisfied. They have welcomed this responsibility because we have also provided them with the tools needed to successfully improve service.

I hope that this letter captures my enthusiasm for our "Journey to World Class Patient Satisfaction." For us, it has been a sound business decision, and it has improved patient satisfaction and employee morale. The role that you have played in this effort is invaluable.

Sincerely,
David B. Tillman, M.D.
President and CEO

Chapter Ten

DEFINING EMPLOYEE CULTURAL EXPECTATIONS

Let's set the bar high. Let's define our vision as "creating world class employee satisfaction."

If "world class" is truly our destination, then a solid foundation for the vision would be to define employee expectations ... and meet them.

Let's begin with you. What do you expect as an employee? How do you want to be treated by your manager/boss?

Listed below are the answers I have received from thousands of participants in my "Keep your Healthcare Professionals for Life Seminars."

How about checking off the answers you agree with

What do we expect as employees?

- ❐ We want to feel valued.
- ❐ We want to be trusted.
- ❐ We want to be listened to.
- ❐ We want to be respected.
- ❐ We want two-way communication and to be treated as an insider.
- ❐ We want honesty.
- ❐ We want to be paid market value.
- ❐ We want to feel connected.
- ❐ We want fairness.
- ❐ We want to feel supported even during cutbacks and tough times.
- ❐ We want to be recognized.
- ❐ We want to be mentored.
- ❐ We want to be treated consistently.
- ❐ We want growth opportunities.
- ❐ We want to be challenged.
- ❐ We want to be held accountable.
- ❐ We want fair expectations.
- ❐ We want you to let us do the job.

What do these expectations add up to? Employee satisfaction!

I have a series of questions I like you to consider as a result from this expectation exercise.

Question #1: Can you name 3 employees that have consistently met yours or anyone else's expectations as noted above?

1. _____
2. _____
3. _____

Most people have difficulty thinking of even two.

Question #2: Do you meet your people's expectations? If you answered yes, how do you know?

Question #3: What is the point of making this list? Perhaps if this is what we expect, then maybe this is what we need to provide our direct reports.

Question #4: What would be the value if you and your fellow supervisors, managers, directors and administrator all understood these expectations and made a collective commitment to deliver them and make them part of your every day culture?

Answer:
1. People would look forward to coming to work.
2. Employee morale would go up.
3. Staff turnover would go down.
4. You would develop a reputation that would attract potential new hires.

Question #5: What if you don't succeed in consistently meeting your employees' expectations?

Answer: You may just keep getting what you have got or worse.

I reached three critical conclusions from this discussion:

Conclusion #1 – We are either part of the solution or we are part of the problem. Either we are proactively contributing to our people's quality of work life experience or we're taking away. There is no neutral in the game of leadership.

Conclusion #2 – Employee satisfaction is a passion for the intangibles. If we look at this expectation list, with few exceptions, it is a list of intangibles, most of which cost nothing but are prized so highly.

Conclusion #3 – "Your people are your greatest asset and #1 priority." Without them, what have you got?

Conclusion #4: - In the world of mediocrity, if you'll just meet and manage your employees' expectations, you'll be a star and nobody will be leaving.

So again, don't forget to:

1. Ask everyone. If you were going to leave, what would be your number one peeve? And if they reply, "I'm not leaving." Ask it again and keep asking until they give you an answer.

2. Do you reserve the right to change your mind?

3. What would cause you to change your mind?

E =

Empowerment

is the Way

Chapter Eleven

UNLOCKING THE MYSTERY OF EMPOWERMENT

"The world is round, and the place, which may seem like the end, may also be the beginning."
Ivy Baker Priest

I had to fly out of Los Angeles and when I showed up at the ticket counter, the airline agent greeted me with the usual indifference. Then a co-worker interrupted to speak to the agent, who then was suddenly nice to me.

She asked, "Mr. Lee, are you going up to the departure gate right now?" I replied, "As a matter of fact, I am." She continued, "We have two physically impaired customers that need to have their tickets changed. It's a long way to the gate and we just don't have the staff or time. Would you mind taking the tickets up for us?" "Sure. You can trust me," I said.

I have this little ritual when I depart from Los Angeles International Airport (as any airport for that matter). I like to arrive at the airport early to avoid stress. I pick up my ticket and go through security, stop at the newsstand to buy a copy of USA Today, (which is my comic book), and the Wall Street Journal. If I'm in a good mood, I'll get another magazine like Forbes or Fortune. My next stop is the men's room (a traveler can never pit stop too often). I then make my way over to Starbucks. There I get my Grande, decaffeinated, low-fat, sugar-free latte, extra hot. And if I'm in a good mood, I'll get a low-fat, poppyseed muffin. Then I dart for the gate and I'm in seventh heaven. I get to read my paper, uninterrupted, and enjoy my gourmet refreshments.

Today is different. I've been empowered. I head through security but now I'm a man with a mission. While I see the beckoning newspaper headlines, I walk past the newsstand. I march past the men's room. I smell that waft of heavenly odor coming from Starbucks but I keep going. I arrive at the departure gate, put the ticket down, and eagerly announce, "Brian Lee reporting, there's your tickets ma'am!" The departure gate agent replies, "Thank you."

What the hell happened? How did I become a volunteer employee for an airline that I don't really care about? I had been given responsibility. I had been given authority and I had been trusted. I was empowered--paycheck or no paycheck.

Empowerment Defined. One of the definitions of empowerment that I would like to share with you is... "Seeing the best in others, helping them see to it themselves, and holding them accountable for results."

Please understand that if you are going to grow your people into accountable adults, who take greater responsibility and ownership, personal change and growth may be needed. Eighty-five percent of the people that work for you have self esteem issues. How do I know? I did myself. When I was in grade 10, I had an inferiority complex. My mother was on welfare and my prospects were not very good. And on top of that, I had no second parent.

I ran for public office at a very early age because I wanted the whole world to say, "Brian Lee, you are okay, even if you don't have a father, you're okay." I want to tell you politics is the wrong place to go for approval. We are all in search of affirmation in our lives so you need to show your people that you believe they are capable of more.

To begin with, you need to believe in them. They need to believe in themselves and their own capability. They need to know you have confidence in them.

Another definition of empowerment is "delegating power to satisfy the customer for the customer's convenience, not yours."

Still another definition is "giving responsibility, granting authority and requiring accountability." Now I have noticed that, as managers, we are pretty good at granting responsibility but we don't do a very good job of giving our people the authority necessary to go with responsibility. Yet we still hold them accountable for results." Anita Roddick, founder of The Body Shop, says a good definition of empowerment means, "each staff member is responsible for creating their organization's culture." I like that. That to me is the ideal...where each employee understands it is part of their job to make sure the culture they work in is a positive, supportive environment.

10   9   8   7   6   5   4   3   2   1

I have a question for you in terms of your people's potential. I want you to circle and rate the overall utilization of their potential on a scale of 1 to 10 with 10 being high, 1 being low and 5 being somewhere in between. So for the people that work for you and with you, the people that you know about, how much of their potential productivity are you getting everyday? Just pick a number and circle it (there is no right or wrong).

Okay, let me ask what you feel you are getting ... is it a low 1 out of 10, 2 out of 10, 3..., 4..., 6..., 7..., 8 ... 9.... 10? Now what would you think is the overall average after surveying literally thousands of managers? It's between a 5 and a 6.

Is there an opportunity here to improve? You bet there is. And the opportunity is not just greater productivity for the good of the organization. The opportunity is to help your people to move closer to their God-given potential, to experience their career and life to its fullest.

Think about the days that have been most satisfying for you in your life. It was when you contributed the most you could, wasn't it? Because when we are giving, when we are contributing and stretching and doing the best we possibly can, that is when we fully utilize our intelligence, our creativity, our knowledge, our wisdom, and we are truly experiencing life to its fullest. And when we don't show up fully, what real satisfaction can there really be?

So I want to ask you 2 questions.

Question #1: Do you value your people as your greatest asset? Just think about that. What do you see when you look your people in the eye? Do you see capable, committed, intelligent individuals who in their own personal life, make sound decisions, exercise good judgement, and do so in their professional career? Or do you see people who need to be stood over and told what to do?

You see there are two theories of management: theory y and theory x. One theory says people are well motivated and the other says people are not well motivated. I have a question for you. Which theory is true? I also have an answer for you. Which ever theory you believe to be true is true, with the exception of losers. A loser, by the way, is a human being that won't live up to their God-given potential. A manager in one of my seminars once told me that she has "excellent people." They just don't act "excellent!"   But other than that, which theory is true? Whichever theory you believe to be true is true.

I was speaking in Sydney, Australia a few years ago, where they had just opened a prison. I read an interview with the superintendent, Mr. Routley, who stated, "if prisoners come in as an idiot, they will be treated like one." Now my question is, do prisoners come in as idiots then treated like idiots? Or do they come in as human beings, get treated like idiots and then, thanks to this self-fulfilling prophecy, they become idiots?

Except we are not talking about prisons here. We're talking about your people. The critical concept I want you to get here is that people will almost always live up to your expectations. My mentor, Roy Wilson, who just retired recently, believed in me and believed there wasn't anything that I could not do. And guess what I wanted to do for him? Anything, because he believed in me.

Do you remember someone like that in your life? That you just wanted to do anything you possibly could because they were on your side? They were your champion...your cheerleader. Perhaps it was a teacher or maybe a grandparent. We love grandparents because they don't judge us. We need more people like them.

I had one manager say to me on one occasion, "Well Brian, I have high expectations of my people and they always disappoint me." What would it be like working for someone who was always communicating a message of disappointment? I'm certain that, after a while, most people would say, "If you are going to be disappointed, I'm going to give you something to be disappointed about!"

One young man told me that he had worked in a bottle depot and his boss kept telling him that he couldn't do his job right. After a while he told me he was literally making mistakes to prove to his boss right.

Sooner or later even the most positive person is going to give up if they are not getting positive affirmations combined with positive expectations.

Here's a tip: Take a look at the productivity of your people and then take a good look in the mirror. Is it a coincidence or do your people's results have anything to do with your expectations?

My next question is who can be motivated? Answer? Nobody! I'm here to say that you cannot motivate another human being.

You say, wait a minute, wait a minute, this book is supposed to teach me how to motivate. Where did you ever get the idea that you can motivate another human being? Have you ever belonged to a union? If you did, then you might recognize the term "work to rule." Work to rule generally means that employees follow the exact rules to the "t" and that means little, if anything is going to get done. At the minimum it results in a work slow down.

My question for you is: can you be forced to work hard if you don't want to? Can you be forced to care if you don't want to? Can you be forced to think if you do not want to? I'm curious to know what you can be forced to do? Show up! Think about it. The fact is, you're going to do what you want to do, for your reasons, not mine. When you sign off from one of my e-seminars, it doesn't really matter what I say beforehand, you're going to do what you want to do for your reasons, not mine!

So what's the answer here? Dr. Madeline Hunter of UCLA said, "You can lead a horse to water, but you can't make it drink. However, you can always salt the oats." So what's your role in creating an environment in which people want to contribute? Fundamentally the beliefs, values and habits, both good and bad, that people have invested a lifetime acquiring, are going to come with them, and that is what you get. So what does that say about the importance of choosing new employees with care? Everything! Since people are going to do what they want for their reasons, not ours, maybe it would be a good idea to figure out what their reasons are? In other words, what makes them tick? We will, by the way, be covering this subject in great detail a little later. Which leads me to our next topic. What are the three general primary human motivators? Well if you read Abraham Maslow, it's food, clothing, and shelter. Although, if you look at the way people really spend their money, it is food, liquor, drugs, clothing and shelter!

But what are the three motivators? Let me encourage you to write them down. Number one is fear. If you don't do it, I won't like you. If you don't do it, I won't love you. If you don't do it, I won't hire you. If you don't do it, I won't give you a raise. I won't love you or care about you. It is called the stick. If by chance you happen to have children, you may have some first-hand experience with the use of this emotion called "fear." Does fear work? Yes, it does. For how long? I've been told not long enough.

The next motivator is reward. If you do it, I will like you. If you do it, I will give you a cookie. If you do it, I will care about you. I will protect you. I will promote you. I'll give you a raise. Does reward work? Yes! For how long? Not very long! How long did it take you to spend you last raise? What happens when you run out of rewards? You've got a problem. We call this "the carrot."

But I want to suggest to you the primary motivator. The one that causes people to move mountains, leap over tall buildings and do incredible, impossible things. I want you to think about those times in your life when you have accomplished achievements that were important to you; when you aspired to an important goal and reached it. You did it because of this and it is one simple word. The word is choice. Please write that down. Make a choice to do what you want to do for your reasons, not anybody else's. Where you accomplished something significant, not because your parents wanted it for you, not because your spouse wanted it for you or your boss wanted it for you, but because you wanted it for you.

So what does this insight then say about the way we need to deal with and communicate with our employees? My conclusion is that if we want staff to own the problem and the solution then we'd better give them the opportunity to make choices... the same way we have. That means we have to spend more time giving them information on the big picture, and above all, explaining the how and the why. "If you were me, what would you decide?" We have a crisis here. What should we do? "If it were your decision, what would you do?" It means we have to stop talking down to them as if they were children. We have to talk to them adult to adult. "Here's the situation."

I would like you to jot down and guess what you think really motivates people. Give yourself one minute. I want you to guess what you think are the three major motivators for front line employees.

_____

_____

_____

I want to share with you the results of a study that was conducted by Kenneth Kovach at George Mason University. I've seen 20 similar surveys, in which, almost all substantiate this one.

Managers thought the following were the most important: Money, Job Security, and Promotion Opportunities.

I have a few questions for you. How much control or influence do you have over the money your people get paid? Virtually nothing. Who decides that? The employee does by their education, experience and attitude. Ultimately the job market establishes a "market value" for every occupation. If you significantly underpay your staff, your turnover rate will skyrocket.

If you significantly overpay, you'll eventually become uncompetitive and go broke. Next is job security. How much control or influence do you have over job security? Who decides that? Your people do by the attitude and skill they bring to their job. While union agreements and policy may create exceptions, few organizations today can afford to keep unproductive staff very long.

Number three is promotional opportunities. Now this is interesting. While managers do have some influence and ability to choose or recommend, in reality, most managers really do have to promote the best person for the job and that ultimately is a function of each individual's personal initiative.

Next, I want you to take note of the three motivators employees said were most important: Appreciation, Being an insider, Empathy for them as human beings.

Question - How much influence do you have over the appreciation you show your people? Answer: A lot!

Next question. How much control or influence do you have over how you communicate with your people and make them feel like an insider? Answer: Almost 100%.

Final Question. How much control or influence do you have over the empathy you give them as human beings? Answer: Complete Control.

Now there was a lady in my seminar that came to me and said, "This is all very nice Brian, but I really deserve to be paid $1000 a month more." I said, "I tell you what, if I was able to get you a $1000 a month raise, would you work any harder?" She replied, "No, but I deserve it."

Now, let's put things in proper perspective: If you were to go to an employee and ask them what it takes to motivate them, what do you think they would say? Of course they are going to say, "pay me more." But the key here is, we have to pay people within plus or minus 10% of the going rate in the marketplace. There is no way around paying competitive wages or salaries. It is possible to keep people who could make more money elsewhere, but that usually only happens if the job and work culture is an environment the employee looks forward to going to everyday. And so much of that, as we've just learned, has something to do with you and the leadership you provide.

Chapter Twelve

THE SIX STEPS OF EMPOWERING LEADERSHIP

In your role as a leader, there are only two jobs that really matter

JOB #1: *Keep the customers you've got (the fact is - the average business loses half its customers every 5 years).*

JOB #2: *Keep the good people you've got. The cost of replacing a valued employee is 150% of their annual compensation.*

So to simplify job #2, which makes job #1 possible, I will summarize for you the 6 steps of empowering leadership:

1. Choose well.

2. Train well.

3. Give people the tools to do the job.

4. Get out of the way and let people do their job.

5. Be a coach, counselor, champion resource, mentor and cheerleader.

6. Recognize, celebrate and continuously educate.

So lets go back now and study each of these steps.

Step #1 Choose Well. Do we really choose well? This is a critical area - we must get really good at hiring great people. One great person is worth three average people. Unfortunately, we often spend too little time selecting the right person for the job, then end up spending way too much time fixing the mistakes.

Step #2 Train Well. The key here is to get better at orienting new employees as soon as they start, especially to the department or work unit.

Step #3 Give people the tools to the do the job. There is no shortcut here. Your staff must be well-equipped. A key tool here is training.

Step #4 Get out of the way and let people do their job. Instead, managers meddle, control, irritate and discourage. It's called the "Dilbert Principle."

Have you ever read Dilbert? The Dilbert principle is this: You take people who have nothing to contribute and you put them in a place where they will do the least harm ...management. Since they don't know what to do, they spend too much of their time meddling with dumb ideas. One of my favorite Dilbert cartoons has the boss pontificating at the head of the board room table. "I've been saying for years that our most valuable asset is people. It turns out that I've been wrong. Money is our most valuable asset. Employees are ninth. One of his lowly employees, seated to the boss's right, blurts out, "I'm afraid to ask what was number 8?" The boss replied, "Carbon paper."

Step #5 Be a Coach. Coaching is such an important skill. Do you value and appreciate the key elements of effective coaching?

Step #6 is recognize, celebrate and continuously educate. Instead we too often ignore. We like being liked and appreciated. We dislike being disliked but we loathe being ignored. We can't stand it. What is one of the worst things you can do in a relationship? Walk away in the middle of an argument. "Don't you walk away from me when I'm telling you off! " Or, if you really want to make the ones you love crazy - hang up while they're talking on the phone! That's downright evil, especially if they don't know where to call you back!

In the past two chapters, you have learned that the motivators that really count with your employees are appreciation, being treated as an insider, and empathy for your people's problems. These are totally within your control and influence.

To sum up, I have a few action recommendations for you and I encourage you to take them back to work with you to try them out, right away.

1. To begin with, see your people as capable, intelligent individuals and communicate positive, supportive expectations that they can learn, grow and be empowered.

2. Do whatever it takes to get good at rewarding the best of the best by utilizing a personnel-selection-profiling tool

3. Whenever possible, initiate procedures to permit a small group of employees to interview, choose and/or make the final hiring/selection recommendations from a short list of employee prospects. You'll find this will result in better choices and your staff will not only be honored that their input matters but you'll find them more supportive and helpful in orientating and training to retain this new hire.

4. New hires are at their best and are the most enthusiastic they'll ever be during their first 10 days. Initiate a process to ensure a quality new hire orientation process, including, at the very minimum, the use of a positive buddy and/or mentor system.

5. Above all, treat your staff as adults. Give them the gift of adulthood by explaining the "why, and "how" whenever you can. If possible, encourage them to participate in decision-making. To do this, it's your job to keep them well informed.

6. To ensure your pay level is appropriate, conduct a semi-annual compensation survey and make sure your mid-range is what your competitors are paying.

7. Keep uppermost in your mind that workers are motivated primarily by appreciation, empathy for them as individuals and being treated like an insider.

8. Focus on your 2 critical jobs as a manager:

   – Job #2 is keeping the good people you've got.

   – Job #1 is keeping the customers you've got.

9. On a continuous basis, make sure your people have the tools they need to do the job.

10. Master the art of coaching.

Chapter Thirteen

FIVE EMPLOYEE ATTITUDES

Question: Which are you?

I have a question for you. Does everyone have the same positive attitude as you do? I don't think so.

Let's take a look at and understand the 5 types of employee attitudes.

They are: Superstars, Winners, Grinners, Sinners and Slugs. The following describes each of these attitude types in great detail.

The first group is Superstars. They comprise about 3% of the work force. They will rise to the top wherever they go.

The next group is Winners. They're positive. They contribute and they want the organization to succeed. They'll come early and leave late. They want to progress. They want to get ahead and above all, they want to make a difference.

The Five Employee Attitude Profiles

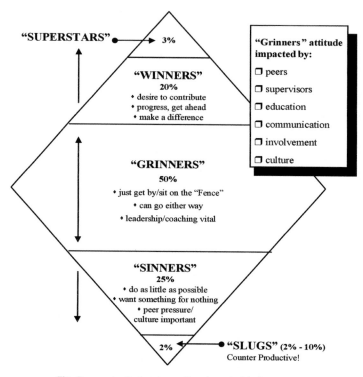

This diagram visually depicts overall worker attitude/values towards their employment/career.

Attitude-diamond.ppt

The third group is called Grinners. Please understand the vast majority of the working population is sitting on the fence, waiting to be influenced and led. They can go either way. The reason I call them "Grinners" is they come to my seminar, smile at everything I say, then go back to work and do exactly what they did before.

The fourth group is called Sinners. They do as little as possible. They want something for nothing. They come late and leave early. They use all their sick time, and can be heard saying, "that's not my customer; that's not my job." They are often openly hostile to management and they brag about it at coffee. They will challenge you in front of others.

The fifth and final group is the worst group. We call them Slugs. They make up anywhere between 2%-10% of your work force. They ought not to be working anywhere, but we keep them working because they are a live warm body. We keep them working because the only way to get rid of them is to accurately and consistently document their inappropriate behavior, which is an awful lot of work and may actually require performance reviews to be completed on time.

Besides there's a better way to get rid of them. Just transfer them. One manager calls it, "pass the trash"; especially when there's an unsuspecting new manager in a neighboring department. We keep them working for us because we do not want to burden the state with additional welfare. We keep them working for us because we don't have the courage to do what is required.

Now the fact that the bottom two groups even exist and get away with their negative and toxic attitude, what does it say to everyone else? That it's OK. Well, it's not OK. It's especially demoralizing to their co-workers.

Your role is to remove the bottom tier, legally terminate them and support them to get on with their lives...some other place, not at yours.

So what's our goal here? To grow the Grinners into Winners through the process of positive peer influence. We're going to grow them into winners through your role as a positive empowering manager. We're going to help them evolve into winners through continuous education. We're going to grow them into a better attitude with high quality communication that comes from you and your leadership peers. We're going to grow them into Winners through involvement, by making them part of the solution rather than staying as part of the problem. We are going to permanently change the culture when we make these changes.

What's our goal with the Sinners? Get them to shut up and do their job! They have to receive a crystal clear message, that it's no longer OK to be openly negative.

For those of you who are not quite sure how to terminate the slugs, there are entire manuals available in "best practice termination." Make sure you connect with your Human Resource Manager or consultant on this topic. He or she will know exactly what to do and how to advise you on these sensitive topics. But ultimately, it is your job, not theirs.

My next question is, which one of these attitude profiles are you?

To summarize, here are three "D.O. I.T." Recommendations

1. Focus on growing your "grinners" into "winners."

2. Make sure your "sinners" understand that a negative attitude is not acceptable and incorporate this approach into your performance review process.

3. Successfully, legally and effectively remove chronically non-productive staff. In other words, support your "slugs" to get on with their career some place other than working for you.

Chapter Fourteen

THE 12 IMPERATIVES OF EXCEPTIONAL EMPLOYEE MORALE

Growing up in Winnipeg, Manitoba, where winters are known to be brutally cold, my buddy and I used to play characters from a famed television series. I was Don Diego de la Vega, better known as Zorro. My friend was Zorro's devoted servant, Bernardo. Together, we'd don our parkas and go fight as lonely spirits against all the gangs and ills of the world. After awhile, a third fellow joined us, then a fourth, then a fifth. By the end of the year, nearly everyone in our school was part of our troop. At the time, I didn't realize I had natural leadership abilities and that people wanted to play with me. That's what leadership is. "The art of inspiring others to play your game."

Morale is a "feeling or mood."

Imperative is "an absolute must."

I know a wonderful nurse leader at Hoag Hospital who implements all kinds of team building activities for her staff. Her department has become a cooking club and have frequent potluck dinners. They play together...even games on night shifts. People do not want to leave her department and there is a waiting list to get in. Her secret? She makes the job fun and she makes it a number one priority.

The benefits of high employee morale are self-esteem, increased productivity, employee retention, better outcomes, increased patient satisfaction and people who really like to come to work. The barriers to morale are slugs, sick call, stagnation, not enough time, negative leadership, patient complaints and the past history—people remember everything.

I have two questions for you:

Question #1. Are you interested in receiving feedback from your staff about what they like about the leadership you provide them?

Most supervisors and managers usually reply yes.

My second question is, "Would you be interested in receiving feedback about what your staff doesn't like about your leadership?"

Interestingly enough, when I ask an audience of managers, almost everyone replies firmly, "yes!"

When I ask them, "why?" the unusual reply is, "so we can improve and get better!"

So in the spirit of continuous improvement, I challenge you to utilize this Leadership Empowerment Survey twice during the next year.

Let's take a look at the survey form.

Please note the word "confidential" at the top of the page. It's critical that each respondent feels confident that his or her input is absolutely confidential, otherwise all you will get is political posturing.

All they need to do is print the name of the manager/supervisor they report to and date the form.

The instructions then reads as follows:

The Service Excellence Semi-Annual
Leadership Empowerment Satisfaction Survey

CONFIDENTIAL

To assist your leadership team in its mission of creating a "customer driven culture through people empowerment", we sincerely appreciate your completion of this confidential survey and forwarding it to the location and deadline noted below. PLEASE DO NOT IDENTIFY YOURSELF IN ANY WAY. Thank you. After each question, the respondent is asked to use a 1-5 rating scale.

5 – for Always   4 – Usually   3 – Sometimes   2 - On Occasion and 1 – Never

Let's quietly review these 10 common-sense questions.

The Leader I report to:

1. **Respect**

   Treats me with courtesy, dignity and respect.

2. **Communication**

   Encourages open, honest two-way dialogue and actively listens.

3. **Alignment/ Trust**

   Leads by example and practices what they preach (i.e. customer driven, continuous improvement).

4. **Recognition/ Feedback**

   Values my contribution and recognizes service "above and beyond."

5. **Empowerment**

   Involves, consults with and empowers me. (Empowerment - "gives me sufficient authority to satisfy my customers in a timely way").

6. **Insider/ Information**

Keeps me well-informed about changes so that I truly feel like a knowledgeable "insider."

7. **Coach/ Champion**

Is an effective coach, who adapts their leadership style to my unique needs and helps me see the "Big Picture."

8. **Training/ Tools**

Ensures that I have the tools and training to do my job in a timely and effective way.

9. **Leadership**

OVERALL, I rate my satisfaction with the leadership provided as:

10. **Friendship/ Empathy**

PS I really look forward to coming to work.   Yes or No

The survey form concludes by inviting the respondent to "Please insert into a Confidential Envelope and return it to" a predetermined location with a specified deadline.

During the past decade our clients have received and completed literally hundreds of thousands of these survey forms, and here's what we've learned from the results.

The key here is to look at the overall average from question #9, and /or the combined average of all 9 questions.

- **A 4.5 to 5 is Excellent.** Keep up the great work and keep sharpening the saw.

- **A 4 to 4.5 is Good.** I recommend picking the one or two questions you scored the lowest on and giving them extra attention.

- **A 3.5 to 4 is borderline OK**, however, you probably received a very low score in one or two questions, which means those areas will need your priority attention.

- **A 3 to 3.5 is poor.** I strongly recommend you make every effort to put to work what you have learned in this book. I also recommend you consider one of the immediate actions.

1. Obtain a personal coach.

2. Invite a seasoned manager who received a 4.5 to 5 score to become you mentor.

- **A 3.0 or less should set off alarm bells** that whatever you're doing is not working very well, or not at all.

In addition to obtaining a personal coach or mentor, an immediate meeting with your supervisor or Human Resource Manager is recommended.

To assist you in leveraging the full value of this survey, I'd like to share with you a tip on how to administer, summarize, and utilize the information provided.

1. I recommend the survey be given to all staff to rate all of their individual managers at the same time. If this is not possible, then please do proceed to conduct your own survey.

2. Pre-arrange for someone to completely collate the forms. This should be someone within your organization that is perceived to be objective and independent. A second alternative is to get someone from outside your organization to do it.

3. Give a copy, along with a pre-addressed envelope to every direct report. Please note that you must have a minimum of 5 participants or respondents may suspect the confidentiality of their reply and give you a whole wash.

   If you have fewer than 5 direct reports, then I suggest you ask other individuals, with whom you work closely, to evaluate you. That means some people may complete more than one form.

4. When you give out the surveys, ask your people to return it to you, an alternate person or locations in a sealed envelope before the end of the day. It only takes a minute or two to complete.

5. Remind them, as it is stated on the form, not to identify themselves in any way.

6. If you are not happy with the results, I caution you not to reflect that negatively to your people in any way or you'll undermine the future use of this process.

7. In the past, I've observed that the managers who benefit most from the survey process initiate an open dialogue with their staff about the question results with the lowest scores and make every effort not to be defensive.

8. As a guideline, I recommend this survey be done twice a year.

9. Your goal should be to improve your overall average by one rating level every 6 months. If you're already in the 4.5 – 5 "A" category, then any improvement would be positive.

In closing, I trust you will find the Empowerment Survey a useful tool for personal and professional growth. As Ben Franklin once said, "Feedback is the Breakfast of Champions." It was also Ben Franklin who said, "That which is painful, instructs." If you do accept my challenge to use this survey, I predict you'll find it a valuable and helpful new tool that instructs.

Chapter Fifteen

RESPECT

"No leader can be too far ahead of his followers."
Eleanor Roosevelt

Common courtesy shouldn't be so uncommon that it is mistaken for genius. Respect is independent of how hard you ask someone to work. Respect is knowing what's important to people. It's an attitude that can't be taught.

When anyone came to see my mentor, Roy Wilson, they would also see his assistant sitting at her desk. Whenever a guest would leave his office, Roy would introduce him or her to his assistant. If the visitor already knew who his assistant was, why bother? It shows respect. If you tour someone through your department, you should also make every effort to say something about each individual who works there. Respect says, "I value you as a person."

Here is a list of some of my favorite ways to show respect:

1. Use their name.

2. Make them feel like an insider by keeping them well informed. Above all, avoid the "Mushroom Technique." Don't keep them in the dark and cover them with manure.

3. If someone calls in sick, give him or her a call to sincerely and empathetically see how he or she is.

4. Recognize and understand the workload. Personally lend a helping hand if they appear overwhelmed.

5. Eye contact.

6. Ask for their input with decision making.

7. Remember their birthday.

8. Recognize the anniversary of the day they began working for you.

9. If they're are a member of a minority group that celebrates special cultural days, make sure you let them know that you are aware of them. For example, members of the Greek Orthodox faith don't celebrate birthdays, they celebrate "name days." Every name has a day, and if it happens to be yours, it's a special day, not unlike a birthday. For Muslims, Christmas is not a big day, but Ramadan is. It is amazing how a little bit of acknowledgement goes a long way.

10. Staff socials for appropriate occasions are very important and a lot of fun.

11. Acknowledge their children's achievements.

12. Saying good night at the end of a shift and saying thank you when they are done.

13. If you're going for coffee, offer to bring back refreshments for others. You'll never know when this kindness might pay an extra dividend. I arrived at the airport one day and checked in early. I came to the departure gate, way ahead of schedule, so I decided to go for a

Starbucks coffee. When I go to get a Starbucks for myself, I often feel guilty if I don't offer to get one for someone else, so I asked a lonely looking ticket agent at the departure gate if she was interested. She replied, "yes", with a surprised smile. I proceeded to procure two decaffeinated, non-fat lattes with sugar-free vanilla and gave one to her. Fifteen minutes later, while I was enjoying my latte and waiting to board the airplane, she came up to me and said, "you're Mr. Lee aren't you?" I replied, "yes." She must have picked up my name when she issued me my boarding pass. "I'd like you to have this." She presented me with a ticket, upgrading me to business class! While my gesture had no expectations intended, I must admit, her response was a nice dividend. The key here is to offer to help others unconditionally.

14. Show little signs of respect. For example, if you know you can't give them a raise, give them a meaningful job title. Although most people, including myself, would rather have the raise!

Chapter Sixteen

COMMUNICATION

*"To prevent your people's mood from
turning blue, give them a chance to
let you know what they do."*
Brian Lee CSP

One very powerful way to create positive attitudes and lead
by example is to utilize the leadership empowerment tool,
"MBWA."

MBWA stands for **"Management by Wandering Around."**

MBWA is not walking around, slapping people on the back and
saying, "Hey how you doing? Looking good! How's it hangin'
brother!" That could become accurately described as "BS."

MBWA means taking the time to get to know each individual
staff member, one person at a time. Taking the time to say
hello, know their name; know the names of their children,

grandchildren or special pets. It's taking the time to know that they are single or that she may be a star ballroom dancer, or beach volleyball fanatic or mountain climber. It's making the time to get to know what makes them tick and what is important to them.

MBWA does not mean going around intimidating your staff and issuing threatening statements like "What the hell is going on here?" I worked with one senior manager who's potential presence sent staff heading for the hills because he made a point of noticing what was wrong and finding fault. MBWA is more like asking, "What is happening around here that you'd like me to know about and I can help you with?" MBWA does not mean you interrupt a staff member who's really busy or already with a customer so they can talk to you for your convenience. MBWA means being sensitive to their needs. I had one President say to me, "but I have 1000 employees; how do I MBWA with 1000 employees?" My answer to him is the same as my advice for you. Budget 15% of your time visiting with your people without a specific agenda. So he proceeded to invest an hour a day. Now do you think we're talking about an hour or a minute per person? An average of one minute works just fine. This translates into 50 - 60 people per hour, times 20 days a month - that's 1000 people a month.

What do you feel are the benefits of MBWAing? Here are 15 worth considering:

1. It's a chance for your people to get to know you. How else will they get to know you than by talking to you. And when they do, trust can begin to develop.

2. It facilitates communication. You can identify small problems before they become big problems.

3. It's an opportunity to catch people doing things right or approximately right. You then have an opportunity to spontaneously let people know, especially in front of their peers.

4. Rumor control. You can nip false rumors or destructive gossip in the bud (or you can start a positive rumor that's actually true!).

5. It makes you accessible to your people for their convenience not yours.

6. It develops team spirit.

7. It shows you care.

8. It sets an example for aspiring managers.

9. It may eventually help improve internal processes.

10. You have an opportunity to see and recognize your people's potential.

11. It makes people feel important. Do you have any doubt in your mind that, whatever you do or say (or don't do or say), gets repeated to your staff's family and friends that night at supper time?

12. It decreases the "intimidation factor." As much as we would like to think that we are not intimidating, any manager, any boss can be seen as being intimidating because you have the power. Many staff perceive their boss can make or break new careers or even fire them. They may see you for more than you really are. Our job is to put them at ease. I recall when I was a politician, a constituent came up to introduce his wife to me. He was so nervous, he forgot her name. "Oh Brian, this is...oh...the mother of my 3 children."

13. You can pick up great new ideas.

14. It's an opportunity to do an informed investing of your team's skills.

15. And, yes, it's good exercise!

P.S. Here are a few more thoughts about MBWAing. Samuel Goldwyn once said, "the secret to managing is to keep the guys who hate you away from the guys who are undecided." In addition to MBWAing, you may want to promote an "open door policy", which encourages staff to enter your office at any time, as long as the door is open and you're not already busy on the phone. Just make sure that when they do come to see you, you stop working and give them your undivided attention.

When I was a member of city council I practiced a form of reverse "MBWAing." I wanted City Hall to understand the problems in my area, so I rented a double bus, then took city council and the press on a tour of the neighborhoods in my constituency for three hours. We visited the Greek Church and the senior citizens drop-in center. We toured neighborhoods where the roads were full of potholes. I reaped dividends from that "team MBWAing" for years.

It is very helpful when you visit with your people at their convenience, where they work, not necessarily in your office. Especially if you want to avoid the pitfalls illustrated in one of my favorite cartoons, where an embarrassed manager is seen saying to his employee seated in front of him: "Let me start off by saying this; I called you in here by mistake and I now want you to leave!"

The further you get from the front line, the less opportunity you have to build trust. But be aware. There are three types of communicators:

The Egotist – always talks about themselves

The Bore – always talks about someone else

The Brilliant Conversationalist – talks to you about you

You need to be accountable for 100 percent of your communication. You have to make sure your staff hears you. It they get that perplexed look on their face, you know you have to clarify. "Is there anything you need to ask me about what I just said?"

Management tends to forget what its like on the front line. Any slight, however unintended, will be the subject of discussion at a subordinate's dinner table that night.

If an employee came to see Tammy McMahon, she might say, "I'm busy right now. When can I come to see you?" She makes every individual feel like they are one of the most important people in the world. Everyone wants to be listened to.

I've prepared an outline for you for what I call "one hour of active listening." By way of background, one of my leadership empowerment students was a manager who had just been promoted to manager of a hospital--an admitting department with 40 employees. There were bad vibes and department morale was terrible. Even worse, she had no previous supervisor or managerial experience. She followed the advice I'm about to give to you and enthusiastically reported solid rapport with her people.

I recommend this to new managers and I recommend this if you have been around for a while. If you are not as close or tight with your people as you'd like to be, here is what you do.

Number 1: Establish rapport with a little small talk; a little chitchat.

Number 2: Get to know them. "Tell me about your family. What are your interests, your challenges, and your successes?" Then shut up and really listen. If you sincerely take an interest in another person, within 5 minutes, they'll tell you the most important things going on in their life.

Number 3: Ask about their training and education needs. What's important to them right now in terms of education and continuous learning? I wish my past bosses had taken the time to ask me and stimulate my thinking in that direction.

By the way, be careful about the use of the word "boss." It's a convenient word but boss spelled backwards is "double SOB."

Number 4: Ask them what they want to be doing 1, 3, 5, years from now? Be an "active listener" and offer encouragement. This would be a perfect time to be making notes.

Now many of them are going to say I have no idea, but I would sure like to think about it. This is where you can play a useful role to facilitate their career goals. Some may say I want your job in 3 years.

This is good to know because to be a successful leader, you eventually want people to replace you in your job. Don't you?

Now if they tell you they want to stay at the same job forever, that's a different story and it's perfectly okay.

Number 5: And this is the key question. "If you were me, what three changes would you make to improve customer satisfaction, communication, team morale and employee retention? Keep listening.

When they respond, ask questions, be encouraging and avoid being defensive. Draw more comments and make notes.

By the time you are done, you will know exactly what needs to be done, just add your own wisdom, your own vision, and your own common sense. You will have an absolute sense of what you need to do. You'll know who the winners are and you'll know who the B.S.er's are. That is called leadership.

Number 6: Your final question is: "Is there anything else you want me to know?" I call this the "parking lot question." Have you ever noticed when you have been talking or visiting with someone for a lengthy period of time, just as you're about to leave each other in the parking lot and about to say good bye, they save the most important information for the very last moment. "By the way, I quit." You know you are just about to leave home in the morning to go to work and your spouse says, "by the way. I want a divorce." It's like we save things up because we don't quite know when or how to share the really difficult information, so we say to ourselves, "well I guess this conversation is about over, I better say it right now. Is there anything else? Before you conclude your meeting, make a follow up appointment so you can conduct a "peer audit", the details of which I am going to share with you in Segment #5.

In closing, I promise you extraordinary dividends if you schedule your "one hour" one-on-one meetings. You are going to find this an invaluable opportunity to get in touch and be "in sync."

To sum up, let's review my "Do It" recommendations for you, so that you can give priority attention to giving your people "Inspired Leadership."

1. For the next 21 days, invest a minimum of 15% of your time "managing by wandering around."

2. Within the next 60 days, invest a minimum of 30-60 minutes in "one hour of active listening" with everybody who reports directly to you. Take immediate action on the good ideas and the insights that you've got from this process.

OUTLINE - ONE HOUR OF ACTIVE LISTENING

Name: _____

Date: _____   Time: _____

1. Establish rapport; i.e. small talk

2. Get to know them, i.e.
    - ❒ family
    - ❒ interests
    - ❒ challenges
    - ❒ successes

3. What do you want to be doing 1, 3, 5 years from now?
    What can I do to help?

4. If you were me, what 3 changes would you make to improve customer satisfaction, communication, team morale and peer retention?

5. Give out a copy of "My L.I.S.T." *(List of an Individual's Special Things)*
    Talk about how they would like to be recognized for service above and beyond.

6. What are your training/education needs?

7. Anything else you want me to know?

P.S. Don't forget to ask:

1. "If you were going to leave...What would be your #1 peeve?"

2. "Do you reserve the right to change your mind?"

3. "What would cause you to change your mind?"

Chapter Seventeen

ALIGNMENT AND
TRUST

*"Leadership is the process of creating trust, so
that change can occur."*
Bob Hamaberg, Standard Aero

By utilizing the skills and strategic processes described in this
book, you can build a solid foundation of trust with your staff,
and in so doing, create a reservoir of good will that will enable
you to bring about the change necessary to create a customer
and employee-driven culture.

To better understand trust, let's examine the four pillars
of trust:

- **Acceptance:** We trust people who accept us unconditionally. That's why kids love grandparents.

- **Reliability:** It's the little things that undermine our credibility. Do what you say you're going to do. I read a very popular book discussing how its main character attended dog races in Calgary, Alberta. Well, I live in Calgary and we don't have dog races. So much for the reliability of all the other information in the book.

- **Openness:** We fail to keep 80 percent of the agreements we make in life. We need honesty with information to back up our position.

- **Congruence:** Your feelings and actions should match. For instance if I tell you I respect you but fail to consult with you before changing your schedule, how does that make you feel?

 If you're a senior manager, try taking a sabbatical to work in a front line position. Instead of hiring someone else to replace absent staff, managers should work the shift themselves. This will create a tremendous bond and connection. A personal benefit will be the experience of humility and a greater appreciation for what your front line does. Sometimes we forget what it's like in the trenches.

I recall a time when I was Vice President and General Manager of a retail furniture store. I was fed up with receiving so many customer complaints about furniture and appliances deliveries being damaged. Could our trucks deliver anything without breaking, scratching, or denting? I was whining about the problem at the warehouse one day and a supervisor said to me, "If you think you can do any better, why don't you come out and show us how." I said, "Fine, I will." Three weeks later, I spent my entire day on a truck, delivering furniture as an "assistant driver." My less sophisticated title was "swamper." Well, giving them advance notice turned out to be a big mistake. They took all their problem deliveries such as mega refrigerators, oversized sofas, etc, and put them all on my route. I learned a valuable lesson that day; I learned that furniture and appliances get damaged when they're handled. They're put on trucks and taken off trucks, on elevators, around tight corners, and through narrow doorways. Even with the greatest care, they can get scratched and damaged. I went out for a few beers afterwards with the other drivers. The very next day, I made changes in our four policies as a result. What do think my "frontline sabbatical" did for my credibility and trust with my staff?

By the way, I was tipped one dollar. I posted it and framed it. It read, "On the occasion of delivering a Zenith stereo with Tom Parish, driver, truck number 1B, Brian Lee, Swamper."

When you do this, what kind of feedback do you get from your peers? I'll bet they appreciate the effort.

It not only adds credibility, it builds trust. The message you'll be sending is, "What you do is important." I've heard many, many managers tell me what a valuable wake-up call it was.

Chapter Eighteen

RECOGNITION
AND FEEDBACK

"What gets recognized and rewarded gets repeated."
Michael LeBoeuf

Would you take the next minute or so to imagine the last time you received positive recognition from your boss (or peers)? Specifically think about what you did to receive the acknowledgment.

How were you recognized and how did it make you feel? Did you notice how awkward you felt about being acknowledged? Why do you think that is? It's because we don't get it very often. We have little to no experience in knowing how to be acknowledged. It happens so rarely.

A doctor in my seminar told me one day; "recognition is like spraying perfume. You can't give it out without getting some back." When you give recognition, you can't help but feel a little bit better because you get out of your own way. For another human being, it's the highest form of a relationship.

There was a cartoonist by the name of Webster who would send telegrams to relatives and friends or business associates that said, "congratulations." It didn't say why or how, nor did it explain anything or go into detail. There was just one word, "congratulations." People wrote and phoned him back to ask, "how did you find out?" Well, he didn't know anything. He just knew that every day, people do things above and beyond the call of duty that they never get acknowledged or recognized for.

Michael Leboeuf said, "Things that get recognized and rewarded get repeated." Recognize good behavior and it will get repeated. Recognize bad behavior and it will get repeated. Can anyone with children relate to that? If you don't recognize behavior, don't expect much.

Ken Blanchard, the author of "One Minute Manager", said, "Catch people in the act of doing things approximately right as often as possible." Don't wait until they do it perfectly like you because you may wait a very long time.

Let's take a look at this list of 18 reasons why recognition so important?

1. It makes you feel valued.
2. It motivates by setting an example. If I do that, then get that, then I'm going to do that.
3. It reinforces the behaviors you want to promote and encourage.
4. It has a domino effect; it's contagious.
5. It lowers anxiety, especially for the new employees who need to be validated for doing the right thing.
6. It's oxygen for the soul. It shows that you are noticed.
7. It contributes to the self-esteem of the receiver.
8. It feels good when you do it.

9. It contributes to loyalty and enhances team building. If you want to build a team, acknowledge people for their team contributions.

10. It gives the receiver the feeling that they belong to part of the "inner circles."

11. It increases productivity.

12. It shows and gains respect.

13. It's contagious.

14. It inspires loyalty.

15. It makes it easier to handle constructive criticism.

16. It encourages learning.

17. It enhances job satisfaction.

18. It can make your day!

How can you reward people when you can't give them a raise? What are the things you can do that are important but don't really cost a lot, if anything at all?

Here are 23 cool ways we can reward people without mere cash:

1. Say "thank you."

2. Public recognition: Do it in front of others. There was a m a n ufacturing plant where the supervisor wanted to give everyone new ergonomic chairs, but rather than give them away, he challenged his people to increase their productivity by 10% to earn one. The "winners" were then invited into the president's office and congratulated by him. Then they were invited to sit on their new chair as their boss wheeled them onto the factory floor as they did the "Queen's wave" for their peers.

3. Throw a party and supply food. Armies march better when they're fed.

4. Schedule choice and offer flextime. Give your people work options whenever you can - why not?

5. How about offering a day off with pay?

6. A special parking space.

7. A handwritten thank-you note. By doing these magnanimous little things, we want to get rid of that old cliché attitude memo: "To Employees - new incentive plan, work or get fired." That was my old boss's incentive plan.

   The #1 reason employees leave is lack of recognition. A lack of feeling valued.

8. How about an employee of the month program for your department or the entire organization?

9. Have annual service awards where you recognize people for something other than longevity. I think that's very important.

10. Put their name in the paper.

11. Present them with a special certificate. When I was a member of the Alberta Legislature, which is similar to a US State Senator, the name of my constituency was "Calgary Buffalo." I used to present people with a certificate called "The Loyal Order of the Calgary Buffalo Chip." I was Chief Buffalo Chip Lee. Do you know what a Buffalo Chip is? Let's just say it's a hardened form of buffalo manure.

    We'd put it in a nice frame and affix a gold seal and people loved getting it. Any kind of certificate goes a long way.

I have an interesting question for you. Have you ever flown on the Concorde jet? I was speaking in Europe when my plane was cancelled in London. The only way to get back to New York on time for my next engagement was to fly on a Concorde. It's quite the experience. It's like dining in a French restaurant inside a missile. Enclosed in leather seats, they ask you to hold on to your estate wines as you rocket through the sound barrier. Near the conclusion of the flight, the attendant presents you with a gold cross pen and certificate, (which they should for $4000 one way).

Here's another great example of the price of a simple, yet effective recognition program.

The great management Guru, Tom Peters, did a program for the Oregon Forest Service and he told the story about the "GREU" award. By the way, "GREU", is the last name of the guy who thought up this award idea. It seems they hold a monthly meeting where anyone can get up and present the GREU Award certificate to another employee for service above and beyond. The catch is you only get one certificate a year to give out.

So if you received one, it was a great honor.

12. Send out a press release whenever your people earn a designation or receive recognition through their professional association.

When I became a Certified Speaking Professional they published an article in the local newspaper, Imagine. Being a former politician, it was the first time anyone had anything good to say about me in the local newspaper.

13. Take them for lunch and you pay!

14. How about clothing? A client once gave me a leather jacket and I've never forgotten it.

15. Praise them in front of others.

16. Send them to a course or workshop. Better still, schedule them to take my e-seminar!!

17. Bring them a coffee or (low-fat) muffin.

18. Ask them to tell the story about an accomplishment in front of others, then praise them for it.

19. Give them an even more challenging assignment. How would that motivate? Because it's a very effective way to say, I value you. It also sets a positive expectation for the future.

20. Create a "Hall of Fame" and appoint them to it.

21. Present them with a recognition or service pin. For example, there's only 3 ways to obtain one of these "six star pins": A) Complete the Satisfaction Guaranteed Seminar. B) Do something above and beyond the call of duty looking after a customer, or C) Be the author of the seminar!

22. Tell them you're proud of them.

23. The ultimate recognition may be to promote them!

A recent study by American Express concluded that the 46% of those surveyed said the #1 employee desire is "personal feedback." Good or bad people want to know.

Let's quickly review Skinner's four factors of recognition success:

1. Recognition should be specific. For example, the way you handled that difficult customer was marvelous. Way to go!

2. Recognition, to be effective, should be immediate. We hated teachers who took a long time to mark our grades. Remember in grade 12 when you didn't know if you had a life until at last got back your final results.

3. Recognition should be geared to the individual. I had one employee years ago where just showing up on time was a big deal. I had another employee who could fix a photocopier with a coat hanger and toothbrush.

4. It should be spontaneous. We love spontaneous recognition don't we?

Recognition should be specific, immediate, geared to the individual, and spontaneous.

As an aspiring furniture executive, I recall one occasion when I organized our first "midnight madness" sale. I spent months planning it.

About a week before the sale, the storeowner and I went to a tailor together and I bought 5 suits, jackets, etc, but later got so busy with the sale, I had no time to pick up my new suits. I virtually lived in the store for 48 hours during the sale. It was an incredible event. It was the first time we ever sold a quarter million dollars in one day. The following Monday, the President walked into my office with all my suits, and said, "You did a good job. Here are your suits. They're all paid for." Unfortunately, whenever we were at social functions and I was wearing one of those suits, he'd tell anyone who would listen, "See that suit? I paid for it." So my challenge to you is to upgrade your recognition program and breathe some life into it with your enthusiastic leadership.

P.S. There is a book that is an excellent source of recognition ideas called, "1001 Ways to Reward Employees", by Bob Nelson.

If we are going to recognize people for exceptional service above and beyond the call of duty, should we do it with trinkets and things they don't want and will never use such as baseball caps they won't wear, or t-shirts they don't like? Or should we recognize them in ways that have meaning and significance and are important to them?

One of my graduates told me a story about when she started a new job for a manager in a public relations department at a hospital. Her manager asked her to write out a list of cool "little things" that she liked. As it turned out, one of the "little things" she really liked was jellybeans. A few months, later she stayed and worked quite late, completing a project on an impossible deadline. The next morning she discovered a bag of jellybeans with a little thank you note, acknowledging her exceptional work.

The idea that I want to plant in you is, when you celebrate and acknowledge your people, celebrate and acknowledge them with things that are important to them. If they bowl, get them bowling ball polish, or odor eaters, or a lane pass. Give them something that is important to them to let them know you value and appreciate them, something they can enjoy that tells them you are thinking about them.

There is a cute story about a chief operating officer, whose administrative assistant had worked all weekend on a project, and he wanted to show his appreciation. He knew that she was a dedicated ballroom dancer so he called her into the office, walked over to the CD player, clicked on Benny Goodman and said, "Miss Smith, may I have this next dance please?" He managed to execute one dance number with her, and said, "That will be all, thank you very much." Now I know that in many jurisdictions, human contact with staff may be borderline sexual harassment and illegal, but what do you think that gesture of appreciation meant to her?

We need to acknowledge people in ways that are meaningful and important to them, not in ways that are meaningful to us.

I'm providing you with a little tool I think you'll find pretty cool. It's called "My L.I.S.T.", study for List of an Individual's Special Things. One simple idea that really works is, if an employee wants to acknowledge a co-worker, make a card available, a "Caught in the Spirit of Excellence" card. How about the example of a gourmet coffee coupon, a "dollar card" entitling the recipient to an ice cream or a yogurt? Give it some thought.

To wrap up this discussion we've just had about recognition, I want you to focus on getting rid of the old style, top-down management attitude towards employees. It was best depicted in a cartoon that showed an employee groveling in front of his boss with the caption, "Sir, I would just like to say thanks for not permanently damaging any vital organs when you kicked me around in front of the other employees yesterday. Is there anything I can ever do to repay you?"

MY "L.I.S.T"
(List of an Individual's Special Things)

Date: _____

From: _____

To: _____

To help me get to know you better, please write out a
list of your favorite things, so I can know what makes
you "tick"! Thank you!

1. _____
_____

2. _____
_____

3. _____
_____

4. _____
_____

5. _____
_____

6. _____
_____

7. _____
_____

8. _____
_____

9. _____
_____

10 _____
_____

To sum up, let's review my "Do It" action recommendations I encourage you to put to work right away.

1. Catch your people in the act of doing things approximately right as often as possible. Be sure to model the behaviors that you want to see in others.

2. Constantly utilize and practice your favorite "little signs of respect" we reviewed in great detail.

3. Upgrade, enhance and inject enthusiasm into your current recognition program.

4. If you do not have a Recognition and Rewards Program, appoint a team of front line staff to develop one. Give them a budget and challenge them to run it for the first year.

5. A good idea to maintain a high level of interest in this process is to rotate membership in your recognition and awards team by appointing new recipients (such as employee of the month or year).

6. Seek nominations for staff recognition from customers, peers and managers. How about giving some sort of acknowledgement to a co-worker who nominates their peer as an incentive for others to do likewise.

7. When you do acknowledge your staff, be sure to utilize Skinner's 4 factors of success. Recognition should be specific, immediate, geared to the individual and spontaneous.

8. Distribute a copy of the "My L.I.S.T." form to every direct report. Collect them back and use them.

Chapter Nineteen

EMPOWERMENT

> *"Until your Front Line owns your customer*
> *service problems, you'll never solve your*
> *customer service problems."*
>
> Brian Lee CSP

I was touring St. Mary Medical Center two years after we had begun a Service Excellence Initiative. We helped establish a "Y.E.S. Fund"—"Yes to Excellent Service." In other units or hospitals the Fund has different names like "the Guardian Angel Fund" or the "S.O.S. Fund." Every employee is empowered to spend up to $250 to solve or prevent a complaint or to show human compassion for each experience.

During the time of my tour, I noticed a picture of a woman, Gertrude, hanging on the wall in the Step Down Unit. I asked the nurse manager, "What's this all about?" She explained that Gertrude was a patient at St. Mary for one year and within the past six months, even though she did have family, nobody came to visit her. When her birthday arrived, the staff decided on their own to throw a party for her. They bought her a blouse, a birthday cake and surprised her in the activity room with a teddy bear called "Fuzzy." Gertrude wrote the nurses a note to say thank you and that "it was the best birthday party of her life." How do you think those nurses felt? What a wonderful example of demonstrating the power of empowerment.

Ralph Waldo Emerson said, "Be an opener of doors, for such as come after thee, and do not try to make the universe a blind alley."

In other words, your role as a leader is to grow your people, to encourage them, and "open that door" for them. Now the building block principle I would like to recommend is as follows: to "obsolete yourself by empowering people to replace you."

Many years ago I was active in politics, first as a campaign organizer, then as a candidate for public office myself. I recall that we'd start off on day one with nobody. Then by election night, we might have had five or six hundred people volunteering. My goal was to always be so well organized, that by Election Day, there was nothing for me to do except visit polling stations and pray. I remember being told on Election Day to "get out of here, there is nothing here for you to do." My objective was to obsolete myself so I had the freedom of time to prepare my two speeches for election night. One for winning, one for losing. The sad part about this story was that at the end of Election Day, when our organization was functioning at its absolute peak, we would shut everything down until the next election. The cool thing here is that when your team is empowered and organized, you don't have to shut your organization down, you just keep getting better, and better, and better, and better!

It seems to me that what we should do is delegate the things we don't need to do, to people who are better able to do them, so we can focus on the things we really need to do, which is provide inspiring and empowering leadership.

Zig Ziglar, the Texas motivator and speaker said, "the fastest way to get what you want, is to help others get what they want." That is what I mean about being a cheerleader for your people. Now some of your people are happy where they are, doing what they're doing. Thank God and good luck to them, because we're all looking for that place where we can be happy and satisfied and enjoy what we do. But if you want your people to be a champion for what you want to do, then you must first be a champion for what they want to be.

What I have noticed is, every once in a while, you are going to recruit a superstar. They are going to progress up the ranks very quickly, and your role is to keep encouraging, coaching and mentoring to them to open that door of opportunity as wide as you possibly can. Because one of the things I've noticed is, the wider you open the door, the less likely people are going to want to leave someone who is as supportive as you.

Did you ever have a child that wanted to run away when they were little? And instead of discouraging them, you helped them? In fact, when you packed their suitcase for them, did they actually leave?

Become a champion. Be an encourager, a cheerleader. My question for you is, do your people see you that way, or do they see you as an old style "Boss?" Do they see you as someone that doesn't really care? Perceived indifference can totally undermine any potential for loyalty.

Did you ever wonder why people are loyal to you? It's because you are loyal to them. Every newscast on Mother's Day features an interview with little kids, and the announcer always asks them, "Why do you love your mommy?" Almost every time, what do they answer? "Because my mommy loves me!"

As adults, nothing has changed. We're just older, that's all. We're wearing dad's suits and mom's dresses, pretending we're adults.

By the way, have you ever worried that sooner or later, someone is going to find out that you are not really an adult? That you really have no idea what you are doing? That you are going to get found out? Or am I the only one that ever has these thoughts? This worried me for years. I've now bluffed my way long enough that I have convinced most folks and critters that I've actually grown up (sort of).

Let's take a look now at the 3 Keys to Empowerment.

Number one: Help facilitate personal and professional goals. Do whatever you can to encourage your people to set goals and reach for their potential.

Number two: Replace rules with judgement. I believe this is the key because what we are doing is giving people "the gift of adulthood."

This was best illustrated to me when I was speaking to a group of Credit Union managers in Michigan. I was training them on the subject of empowerment and asked the audience, "Do you do the same thing at your Credit Union as they do at my bank?" They said, "What is that?" I continued, "Even though I have been a customer for five years, and the teller serving me has worked there for ten years, if I want to cash a large check, the teller has to go to the accountant to get approval?" And they said, "Of course we do." I said "Why?" They said, "Control." Where's the control? Have you observed a teller take a check to an accountant? They go over to give them the check then what does the accountant do? They sign it. In most cases they don't even look at it or you.

My twin brother Bruce was an accountant at a bank and I always had my bank account at the branch where he worked. I also noticed that my bank balance fluctuated plus or minus depending on what time of the month it was and how broke Bruce was. Coincidence?

Anyway, I asked Bruce "What did you do when you were presented with checks for approval?" He said, "I looked at the customer to see if they were a crook." I said, "Did you ever see a crook?" He said, "I never saw a crook."

So what does a crook look like anyway? I will tell you one thing; they likely don't wear bow ties. If they do wear a tie, it's probably a boring necktie that everybody wears, so no one will notice. But don't let me get started.

Imagine with me, now that we are working together in the same bank, that I am your manager. I'm now going to empower you. You're now empowered. You can now cash any check that you want without coming to me for pre-approval. In order for this empowerment to be effective and work, there must be three T's in place. What do you think those three T's are?

What did you guess?

The first "t" is trust. The question is: do you wait for someone to be trustworthy or do you begin by trusting them? Now explain this to me, why would an employer give someone keys to the place plus security access yet not trust them? Help me out with that one. Why would you keep untrustworthy people working for you?

What's the second "t"? Take a guess. It's training. What does the bank teller need to know about how to approve a check? Everything the accountant knows? Rule #1 of empowerment is you do not empower someone that knows less than you do. You empower someone that knows more than you do. So make sure that they're trained and knowledgeable.

The third "t" is the interesting one, and the toughest one, so please write this down if you haven't already. It's "transition." Do you think there are people who don't want to be empowered, yes or no? Are there people who are not ready to be empowered, yes or no? Are there people working for you, including yourself, that have had no experience with this thing called empowerment? The fact is, few business, government, healthcare or not for-profit-organizations have had much success in this brand new field of human resource development.

Yes there are people whose only desire is to start work at 9, leave at 5, do their job and collect a regular paycheck. So what do you do with them? We coach them to make the transition to empowerment. For example, they come to you with a problem and say, "Oh great guru, what shall I do? Thou with all the knowledge and wisdom, what shall I do?" And you say, "Well I am, after all, your boss. Leave it with me. I will fix it for you." Then the next employee approaches you "I have this problem." And you say "leave it with me." Still another staff member says to you, "I have this problem." Once again you reply, "leave it with me." What they're doing is bringing you the "monkeys on their back." There was an article in Harvard Business Review, many years ago, on this very subject. Whenever an employee has a problem, it's like they have a "monkey on their back." Except, instead of helping them solve their problem, you let them delegate it to you and transfer their monkey to your back. Instead of being an inspiring, empowering leader, you become a zookeeper. No wonder nobody wants to go into management for fifty cents an hour more.

So what could you say to your staff when they come to you with their problems? How about: "What would you do?" And they say, "Well I don't know." Then I want you to repeat the eight magic words of empowerment and they are: "If you did know, what would it be?" Please write that down. All right? Let's take this idea for a test drive. Ready, when I count to 3, I want you to repeat it out loud with me. 1, 2, 3. "If you did know, what would it be?"

Fifty percent of the time you'll get an answer with a positive practical solution. It's incredible; it's like magic. The key here is to ask sincerely and do it with a straight face. Half the time you won't get an answer, so repeat it a second time. Ready 1, 2, 3, "If you did know, what would it be?" Sometimes at that point they will still say, "Well I don't know." But half the time you will get an answer. By now you're up to a 75% success rate. For those who still haven't given you a potential solution, look them in the eye and say: "Well guess." "Well I can't guess." "Oh come on you can guess." They may tell you: "Look that's what you're getting the big bucks for!"

Now have I got a question for you. If someone, after three attempts to solicit any kind of idea, is not even willing to guess, what are they telling you about their attitude? It's not very positive, that's what. It may not be fixable but hang in there because now I have a question for you. Do people generally know what they should do in a situation when they come to you for approval, yes or no? Probably. So why are they coming to you for approval?

Here are 4 key reasons why staff ask you to make a decision to solve their problems.

1. Because you never delegated to them the authority to decide.

2. To show you that they are doing it.

3. Because they do not want to be held accountable and now you are the decision-maker, so you can have the monkey on your back.

4. Because you have not said to them: you don't need to see me because "that is the way we have always done it; because that is the culture; because that is procedure; because that is our policy; and because that is the way it was done when you got promoted."

Now after all this, the second time they come to see you and tell you they've got a problem, you say, "What do you think we should do?" Then they will say, "I don't know", and you say, "Well, if you did know, what would it be?" And they say, "We're not going to do this again are we?" And you are going to say, "You bet we are."

And after two or three times of this, what are they going to figure out? That you trust them, that you believe in them, and that you support them, because in reality, they probably know more about the problem than you do.

They're going to need a little confidence to know that you are sincere about this and that you're not just saying it because you have just taken Brian Lee's seminar and you want to test out a new technique on them. So when should you empower?

There are 9 key barriers to empowerment.

1. When an employee has an attitude that "I do more."

2. Policy that is not understood or has no current relevant reason to exist

3. "Sacred cows": something you do but you don't know why you do it because that is the way we have always done it.

4. When there is a structural problem in the organization's culture.

5. A major burner to empowerment is "F.E.A.R.." False Evidence Appearing Real.

6. A major barrier to empowerment is your people's natural tendency to want to remain in their comfort zone.

7. It therefore follows that the 7th barrier to empowerment is resistance to change.

8. Another barrier is lack of training of how to train others to be empowered.

9. And the 9th barrier to empowerment are self-limiting beliefs, meaning that you either believe that person is not capable or they believe that they are not capable.

So, let me share with you now 12 conditions or circumstances when you know it's time to empower your team:

1. It's time to empower when your customer is annoyed with bad service.

2. It's time to empower when your people are annoyed with dumb situations.

3. It is time to empower when you are consistently rubber-stamping decisions and your people are wearing out the carpet coming back to you again and again while you keep giving the same approval again, and again, and again.

4. It's time to empower when you conduct a process study and identify opportunities to improve efficiency and productivity.

5. It's time to empower when you want to speed up the service cycle. By the way let's talk about this for a moment. Let's go back to the bank. Who wins here, when the teller is empowered to authorize checks? Does the customer win? Yes. Because they experience faster, more timely service. Does the teller win? Yes, because the teller minimizes work interruptions from

running back and forth between the customer and the accountant. Does the accountant win? Yes, because now they have the time to focus on their prime responsibility, rejecting mortgage and loan applications! Does the bank win? Absolutely, because more satisfied customers and a more productive staff means greater profitability. So everybody wins here. Who loses? The thief. I've got a question for you, what is going to happen to the number of bounced checks if tellers are personally accountable for fraud and not the accountant? The number of bounced checks is going to go down.

6. It's time to empower when there is inconsistency in service.

7. It's time to empower when there is a benchmark failure, when productivity is not comparable to similar departments or organizations are just not what it should be.

8. It's time to empower when you are downsizing and getting leaner. In fact, this is a perfect time.

9. It's time to empower when whatever you are doing is not the highest and best use of your time or talent.

10. It's almost an ideal time to empower when you've deliberately changed someone's job description.

11. It's time to empower when you are promoting.

12. And finally, it's time to empower "when in doubt." When you're not absolutely certain it's the right move, take a chance. What do you have to lose? How did you become successful at what you do? ... Through experience? How do you get experience? You make mistakes and learn from them. How did you get so wise? How did you get so omnipotent and knowledgeable? My guess is, by making the odd mistake along the way, just like I did.

During the transition to empowerment, we just have to support our people, that's all.

Now my recommendation here is to turbo-charge your empowerment strategy by implementing a Service Recovery Policy.

Allow me to take some time here to explain this concept. A Service Recover Policy is a policy that is communicated crystal clear to staff, that they have the discretion where there is a service failure, to "recover" in the eyes of the customer. To fix the mistake and solve the problem immediately. If for some reason, they are unable to take action but learn about it after the fact, they can make it right and make a decision on the spot to "dress up" without having to obtain prior approval or permission from management.

Implementing a Service Recovery Policy is achieved with the staff and management applying their "Service Recovery Skills." To simplify this problem, I coined the phrase, "complaint golden rule", which is "Mess Up, Fess Up and Dress Up."

Do we make mistakes? Of course we do. Is there ever going to be a time when we don't make mistakes? Nope!

So when there is a service failure, here are 6 key steps to follow when you or someone else "messes up", which I also teach in the Satisfaction Guaranteed e-seminar.

We're human beings. We're frail. We all Mess Up and make mistakes.

Step #1. Take personal ownership for your customer's problem, concern, complaint or request even if it should be someone else's responsibility. That does not mean you may actually do the work yourself. What it does mean is you stay with the customer until you're satisfied they are going to be looked after. The way I like to say this is "whoever hears the complaint, becomes the customer's saint."

Step #2. Fess up. It's okay to admit that you made a mistake.

Step #3. Sincerely apologize for the inconvenience.

Step #4. Make sure you don't blame anyone else. Don't point the finger at someone else in your organization and blame him or her. First of all, if you make the pointing motion correctly with one extended finger directed at someone else, you may notice that there are also three fingers pointing right back at you! Secondly, does the customer care who's to blame? Nope. All they care about is getting it fixed as soon as possible.

Step #5. "Dress Up." In other words, if an apology or sincere acknowledgement is not enough (and most times it will be), then use your own good judgement based on prior discussion with your supervisor, to make amends for the inconvenience as fast as possible.

"Mess Up, Fess Up, Dress Up." With a few exceptions. If you're a heart surgeon, for example, there might be the odd legal complication as a result of "fessing up." You may want to check with Risk Management.

When you mess up and fess up, dress up by doing something just a little bit more than the customer expects.

Sometimes "dress up" might be just a phone call to ask if everything is okay. Or a handwritten note of apology. All of us can think of something extra, something just a wee bit creative.

For this to happen, it's important that you consult with your fellow managers to agree upon your own Service Recovery Policy and make sure everyone knows about it and uses it.

Practical examples of applying a Service Recovery Policy include:

In a restaurant, empowering staff to write off an entire meal or giving the guest a free desert or liquor.

In a retail store, empowering staff to do alterations at no charge or by personally delivering the product right to the home, discounting the cost or yes, even giving it to the customer at no charge.

To: Brian Lee

From: John D. Mandelker, President

I thought you might want to know how we are progressing as a follow-up to your customer satisfaction training sessions here November 1991.

After your seminar, Streetside Records used and expanded your "License to Please" concepts. We wrote and implemented several customer service courses for our sales staff and managers using the ideas you taught us.

As you can see from one of the customer letters enclosed, we have been able to establish this "License to Please culture" in just a few weeks in Cincinnati.

Your seminar was a catalyst in getting upper management to move and by convincing store management of our serious intent.

Though you may not remember it, at one point you asked a store manager if she would give away a CD to "dress up" a problem. After, she said she would. You asked me to stand up and state my response.

It may have been a little hackneyed but to the managers, it was an epiphany. Yes, we have given away several CD's in the last year (18) but December sales were up 22.9% on a same store basis. Thanks.

In an office, empower staff to provide a bonus level of service or send flowers or a more appropriate serious or humorous gift.

In a hospital or in healthcare, we encourage management to empower staff to use their own discretion to spend up to $250 to solve a complaint, prevent a complaint, or show human compassion. Now in reality they don't need to use their own money because management sets up a voucher system with gift shops, florists, restaurants, and taxi companies, whenever it is necessary. Occasionally an employee might have to go out of their pocket but they know they can obtain cash reimbursement the same or next day.

The problem of implementing Service Recovery has not been staff abusing their authority; the challenge is getting them to use it rather than be worried about making a mistake.

The average expenditure, by the way, is somewhere only between 5 and 20 dollars. The impact is huge, however, in two ways. It is electrifying for frontline employees to know that they are trusted enough to use their own good judgement.

It is also powerful with customers because these are times when their loyalty to you is at risk.

Are you getting excited yet? You should be. This is an exciting concept.

Now that we've spent a good amount of time studying this thing called empowerment, I'd like you to give some thought to how you can immediately apply it to your responsibilities.

What power can you give away? What authority can you delegate, what you do not need to have, to assign to a sub-ordinate? Or if you can't think of anything, what power do you need to get from your manager, so you can be more effective?

Now I now there are some managers who worry that if they give away all of their authority they will no longer be needed.

By the way, have you very heard of or shopped at a department store called Nordstrom?

Nordstrom is an incredibly successful department store that is famous for it's exceptional customer satisfaction. It's especially well known for the quality of its people and to the extent to which they are empowered. Well, I "liberated" a copy of their employee handbook, which is their secret to how they empower their employees to provide such great service. It's pretty cool because they managed to condense what was formerly a 22-page document into one concise paragraph. Are you ready to hear it? Here we go: "Welcome to Nordstrom; we are glad to have you with our company. Our number one goal is to provide outstanding customer service. Set both your personal and professional goals high, we have great confidence in your ability to achieve them. Nordstrom rules: Rule number one: Use your good judgement in all situations. There will be no additional rules."

Nordstrom believes that the worst that could happen would be to have an employee make a mistake in favor of a customer, in which case, they win by earning additional customer loyalty. They realize that occasionally, they will get ripped off but that is the small price they pay for enjoying all the benefits that go with having a world class reputation.

In order to make the transition to an empowering Nordstrom-like culture, there needs to be a transfer of power to the front line. Like the Nordstrom inverted organization chart, which shows management at the bottom supporting the front line staff, who care for their customers, shown at the very top. There are some skeptics who believe that empowerment is just a sneaky way to make frontline employees scapegoats for management problems.

Take a moment now and jot down specific examples of authority that you do not need or that you should get. What can you give away or get today?

Let's take a look at a good example of empowerment. Why not allow staff to create their own schedules? The critical ingredient here is to set solid ground rules, especially for holiday schedules.

It might sound like, "I need the six of you to decide who works Christmas and New Year's but you have to work one or the other." One more example of how you can transfer power. Rotate everyone to take turns chairing staff meetings.

In this chapter you have learned the absolute best use of your time is to make the time to thoughtfully and systematically delegate as much authority as you possibly can to your front line.

To sum up, I have a few action recommendations for you, and I encourage you to take them back to work with you and try them out, right away.

1. Your goal is to "obsolete yourself by empowering your people to replace you" so you can devote your time and attention to leadership communication and coaching.

2. Become a champion for your people's goals and dreams and they will return your support with their loyalty.

3. Wherever and whenever you can, remove unnecessary barriers by replacing rules with judgement by applying the 3 T's of empowerment:

T #1 is Trust ... begin by trusting your people

T #2 is Training... make sure your people know everything you do.

T #3 is Transition... your people can make the transition to be empowered by using the 8 magic words of empowerment, "If you did know, what would it be?"

4. Do whatever it takes to remove and eliminate the 9 major barriers to empowerment which include:

   a) Attitude

   b) Policy

   c) Sacred Cows

   d) Culture

   e) F.E.A.R. - False Evidence Appearing Real

   f) Comfort Zone

   g) Resistance to Change

   h) Lack of Training

   i) Self Limiting Beliefs

5. Look for the 12 primary conditions as indicators when it's time for you to take action and delegate greater authority, including:

   a) Your customer is annoyed

   b) Your people are annoyed

   c) Rubber-stamping

   d) Doing a process study

   e) Speed up service cycle

   f) Inconsistency

   g) There is benchmark failure

   h) Downsizing

   i) Not the highest or best use of your time

   j) I changed its description

   k) Promoting

   l) When in doubt

6. If you don't have one, then make sure your organization has a "Service Recovery Policy" so you can promote and encourage your people to use the complaint golden rule, "Mess up, Fess up and Dress up."

7. Your immediate homework, if you have not done so already, is to successfully change a current policy and/or procedure(s) that specifically gives front line personal (or gets for yourself) greater authority to satisfy your customers in a more timely and appropriate way.

E =

EDUCATION

AND ENGAGEMENT

*"Without information,
people cannot take responsibility ...
with information,
people cannot help but
take responsibility."*

Jan Carlzon

Chapter Twenty

INSIDER INFORMATION

"I have received memos so swollen with managerial babble that they struck me as the literary equivalent of assault with a deadly weapon."
Peter Baida

People can't care about what they don't know about. Most employees would like to be treated as an insider. Wouldn't you?

If something is amiss and management prefers to shield its employees or wait until they have more information before sharing it, chances are the water cooler gossip will spread like a fire in a dry forest, killing morale as fast as burning timber.

What's important for people to know? If you advised your staff on a daily basis about patient satisfaction, their operational budget, and many other issues, gossip, speculation and conventional wisdom would make way for being kept in the loop.

When it come to making your people feel like insiders there are 3 formal and 3 informal approaches.

Three formal approaches include:

Firstly, timely performance reviews that are updated quarterly. Do an annual one, but every three months, let your employees know how they are doing.

Secondly, performance measurement. Let people know what their productivity numbers are. In other words, what are their daily, weekly, monthly sales results or production outcomes.

And thirdly, share with your team how they impact customer service. What are their customer satisfactory measurement scores? What kind of feedback are you hearing from their customers?

Three informal approaches include:

First, one-on-one anything. Any quality contact with each individual is important.

Second, active listening. Actively letting a person know that they are heard. You honor people when you listen to them. Sometimes that simply means asking them how they are, then shut up and just let them get comfortable talking to you.

And the third informal approach is to MBWA.

I want to zero in for a while on the concept of "active listening." There is a huge dividend to be derived from spending quality time with your people. With that goal in mind, I want to recommend to you one of the most powerful, practical tools I can. The concept is called "active listening."

Chapter Twenty-One

COACH
AND CHAMPION

*"To prevent your people's mood from
turning blue, give them a chance to
let you know what they do."*
Brian Lee CSP

If you want people to care about what you want to do, you must
first show them you care about what they want to be.

The most valuable service you can provide your people is to be
their coach and champion to help them aspire to reach their
potential.

Coaching is such an important skill. Do you value and appreciate the key elements of effective coaching? Last October I
decided to take singing lessons. While I can speak to several
thousand people with relative ease, singing in front of a few
people has always been a personal stretch.

In preparing to speak at my church last July; I decided I wanted to sing George Benson's "The Greatest Love of All" as part of my presentation. Since my normal rendition of the National Anthem usually evokes spontaneous laughter from seatmates, I decided it was time to improve my singing abilities.

At my first lesson, I noticed the music studio was lined with six and eight-year-olds. I felt like Adam Sandler in Billy Madison!

It took two months alone just to figure out what key I should sing in. My coach, Karen, would sing a line, then we'd sing it together, and then I would sing it by myself. If I sang it right, she'd praise me. If I didn't, we would repeat the process. Now you have to appreciate that Karen was dealing with one of the most fragile things in the world ... a male ego. She successfully coached me by never making me feel bad or wrong.

Become your people's coach and champion; show them that you care about them and what they want to be. They will return that caring with loyalty.

Chapter Twenty-Two

MENTORSHIP

"Not to transmit an experience is to betray it."
Elie Wiesel

*"Those who don't know what they're doing
are getting rid of those who do."*
Anonymous

As a professional speaker, there is no college or university to attend to become a professional speaker so our professional association created a mentorship program. I enjoy being a mentor so much; I'm currently facilitating four aspiring speakers to move their career along. They receive free advice from me about every conceivable aspect of speaking. I invite them along to speaking engagements with me.

Several years ago, I was a mentor to a young man in Florida. For two consecutive years he spent a week traveling with me as my protegé. A year ago I went to a professional speaker's convention and discovered his speaking fees were greater than mine.

One of the things I enjoy most about being a mentor, is that by giving others advice about what they should do, it reminds me that I should be practicing what I preach.

A study in the book, "Love 'Em or Lose 'Em" by Beverly Kaye and Sharon Jordan-Evans reported that staff turnover was 35 percent with no mentoring but only 16 percent with mentoring.

The word "mentor" originated with Homer's ancient Greek epic, the Odyssey, which details Odysseus' ten-year attempt to return home to the Greek Island of Ithaca after serving in the Trojan War. Odysseus planned the fall of Troy by using the Trojan Horse (a hollow wooden structure that was large enough to hide soldiers inside of it) as a cloaking device. The Greek hero was given the Roman name, "Ulysses", and his most trusted friend and advisor was Mentor. When the adventurer set out his famous wanderings, he left the responsibilities of his household and his son, Telemachus, to Mentor, so he could teach, guide, counsel and oversee.

"Mentors in the workplace can boost young careers but few employees get on-the-job coaching. A U.S. survey by Chivas Regal reports, out of 1,000 people, only 17 percent said they had a mentor. But among those who saw themselves as getting ahead, 76 percent said they had an older, more experience colleague taking a special interest in them. The survey also found that 55 percent of workers felt that senior managers showed little interest in helping younger workers get ahead." Wall Street Journal, May 1996.

> *"A mentor is someone who offers you the wisdom of their years, helps you through the tough times, gives you a pat on the back and helps you target your skills for advancement."*
> Dr. Jan Northup Kratochwill

The benefits to the mentor are personal satisfaction of giving back to the organization; creating a legacy of personal knowledge; career enhancement; higher visibility and prestige; and an insightful reminder of what they should be doing.

The protegé benefits from the assistance in defining realistic career goals; building confidence with encouragement to grow; personalized education; less time spent in the wrong job; plus increased organizational awareness, opportunity for advancement, and leadership abilities.

The organization benefits from a growing "seasoned" work force; increased productivity; cost-effective training; increased organizational communication; motivated employees; strategic planning and succession planning; employee sense of stability; career guidance and effectively integrating new employees into the workplace.

The mentoring process starts with an initial meeting where the objective is for the mentor and protegé to agree upon the process.

Step two is building a relationship to strengthen the mentoring partnership by developing strong communication skills and learning each other's backgrounds and styles.

Step three is strategic planning and commitment...helping the protegé with goal setting.

Next is implementation—achieving the protegé's goals.

The end result is an evaluation to determine how successfully the protegé utilized the information and skills gained in the mentoring process. It also calls for a debriefing and conclusion of the partnership.

The mentor's role is to teach, guide, counsel, and challenge. Asking the right questions, being a good listener, and encouraging feedback are signs of an effective mentor.

THERE ARE THREE TYPES OF MENTORING:

Supervisory Mentoring: This is strictly a working relationship where mentoring is normal function of the supervisor's duties.

Informal Mentoring: Roy Wilson never said to me, "I'm going to be your mentor." But he was. This is an unofficial pairing of two individuals that are drawn together based on chemistry and trust.

Facilitated Mentoring: This is a formal process where a facilitator or coordinator is appointed. It has been shown to be the most effective process of mentoring. It involves commitment from all levels of an organization, as well as from mentors, protegé and supervisors.

For a comprehensive mentoring Tool Kit visit
www.keepyournursesforlife.com, and click on "tool kit."

Chapter Twenty-Three

TRAINING

AND TOOLS

*"The only thing worse than training
your employees and losing them,
is not training them and keeping them."*
Zig Ziglar

*"When your people are learning,
they're not leaving."*
Brian Lee CSP

In the past few years, we have dedicated our training team to deliver the Keep Your Healthcare Professional for Life Service Excellence Initiative. We achieved a breakthrough from 1995 - 1996 at St. Mary Medical Center in Long Beach, California. Rather than teach Service Excellence ourselves and train the managers to do the training, we train their front line staff to do the training.

We named these front line crusaders "Service Excellence Advisors."

We recruited one Service Excellence Advisor (SEA) for every 15 to 20 employees. We didn't focus on just nurses. We included housekeepers, lab technicians...everybody, yes, including doctors.

To be eligible to be an "SEA", we recruited the "Best of the Best" front line stars, who are talented employees with a terrific attitude and who had already demonstrated their customer commitment.

"SEA's" are appointed for a one-year term, serving in this role in addition to their regular job function.

We put them through a two-day "Train the Trainer" course and in the first half-day, we teach them a customer service workshop called "Service Excellence."

For the next day and a half, we teach them how to teach it.

We call the final night's graduation ceremony, "Saturday Night Live." It provides graduates with an immediate opportunity to reinforce and demonstrate their newly acquired presentation skills. Each team of 4 performs a creative skit in front of their managers and family.

I want you to imagine speaking in front of a crowd of over 200 people when you've never spoken in front of an audience before.

The results are always exceptional...This really unleashed front line enthusiasm has a powerful impact on the organization in terms of improving patient and employee satisfaction.

I remember when we first began at St. Mary Medical Center. The culture was ugly. Since then, we had over 300 staff trained to be SEA trainers.

Imagine them teaching a workshop on customer service. And imagine having those same Customer Service Advisors going out into the community to speak to high schools and peers about nursing!

The six roles of a Service Excellence Advisor are:

1. Teaching the Service Excellence workshops to peers
2. Facilitating staff implementation meetings
3. Conducting new hire orientation training
4. Providing a communication link with management to the front line
5. Peer recruitment
6. Serving as a role peer model

To get started, recruit the best of your best front line staff. They will inspire their peers. There isn't a more powerful recruitment program than peers recruiting peers because they believe in where they work and what they're doing.

Introducing...

THE SERVICE EXCELLENCE ADVISOR

"Become the change you want to see in the world."
– Gandhi

Critical Selection Criteria
- Front Line / Non-Management
- Terrific Attitude
- Demonstrated Commitment to Customer Satisfaction

White Memorial / March 1996

Sutter Medical Center / March 2000

Hoag Hospital / April 2000

St. Vincent Medical Center / January 2000

The Keep Your Healthcare Professional For Life™
The Service Excellence Initiative / Year I
The 6 Step Journey to World Class Customer Satisfaction

This Flowchart Depicts the 6 Core Training/Implementation "Steps" of
the Service Excellence Initiative Culture Transformation Process

Who Participates:		**Program Length / Mission:**
Senior Administrators Service Excellence Council (or equivalent)	**Executive Briefing**	3.5 hours **Decision** to proceed or not **Total understanding** of SEI process
(Interval between steps)	*4-8 Weeks*	
1. Entire Supervisor, Manager, "Leadership Team"	**Focus Groups** → **Leadership Briefing™**	4 hours **Buy** in / Commitment preceded by **Focus Groups &** **Interviews** *10 secrets of World Class Service*
	3-4 Weeks	
2. "Leadership Team"	**Service Empowerment Leadership Course™**	2 days Creation of "**Service Leadership Teams**" to proactively be **accountable** for "**changing the culture**"
	3-4 Weeks	
3. **Service Excellence Advisors** **Best of the best,** front-line **Proven** customer **commitment** Chosen for **positive attitude** Ratio of **1 SEA** per 15-20 staff	**Service Excellence Advisor™ Train-the-Trainer Course**	2 or 3 days SEA's **Learn How To:** **Teach** the Service Excellence **Workshop,** Serve as a **Role Model** Conduct **New Hire** Orientation
	3-4 Weeks	
4. Service Excellence Advisors "Leadership Team"	**Winning with Difficult People™ Seminar**	1 day Cope with **Difficult Customers** /Co-Workers Continue **change momentum** **Breakdown** and Elimate "**Us vs Them**"
	2 Weeks	
5. Everyone!	**Service Excellence™ Customer Satisfaction Workshop I**	3 hours/over a 4-6 week period Learn **core skills** of Service Excellence **Attitude paradigm shift** Taught by teams of SEA's x 4 Emphasizes **work unit implementation**
	2 Weeks	
6. Service Excellence Advisors "Leadership Team"	**Just "D.O. I.T."™ Implementation Meetings Facilitator Seminar** / **Service Summit™ #1**	Just "D.O. I.T."™ Seminar – 6 hours How to **facilitate** J.D.I. Meetings (Daily Ongoing Implementation **T**actics) **Service Summit – 2 hours** Service Leadership Teams show- case culture change progress
	7 – One hour Implementation Meetings	
Everyone	① ② ③ ④ ⑤ ⑥ ⑦	One hour work-unit meetings Facilitated by SEAs/Set by Manager **Focus Implementing** Service Excellence Result – 1,000's of 1% Changes
	Every 3-4 Weeks	
Service Excellence Advisors "Leadership Team" Year II SEA Candidates	**Service Summit #II Just "Done It"/Bragg Fair™**	2 hours **Work-units** showcase their enhanced "**Best Practices**" Celebrates **completion** of "D.O. I.T." Phase **Transition to Year II**
Phase II/Year II		**Annual Health Care Service Excellence Conference™**

Chapter Twenty-Four

LEADERSHIP

"Fifty percent of work force satisfaction comes from employees relating with their boss."

Let's begin this chapter by re-defining the difference between "management" and "leadership."

Management is "maintaining and administering the past." We all, as managers, have a "maintenance" role. It's our job to maintain a budget, maintain an inventory, and maintain our customers and staff.

Leadership, however, is "creating the future with and through other people." As leaders, it's our job to create a vision for the future and as leaders, it is our job to create a positive work environment or culture.

The difference is ... Leaders ask, "Am I doing the right things?"

... Managers ask, "Am I doing things right?"

Therefore "Inspired Leadership" is creating an organization future, all through other people, by "leading by example."

Albert Schweitzer said, "Example is leadership." This is why the semi-annual leadership Empowerment Survey that I introduced to you in Chapter #14 is so important.

Our staff meetings at Custom Learning Systems have always been every Monday afternoon. However, if I were going to be out of town, we'd have it the following week. On one occasion, I was literally away for three months. For those three months there were no staff meetings. What happened to employee morale? It tanked. After my return, when we got together for the first meeting, there was a lot of griping to deal with. I made a promise that we would never do that again… wait so long to have a meeting. Today, our meetings are participatory, fun, sometimes intensive, but everybody is part of the process.

As Ben Franklin said, "That which is painful, instructs." Sometimes feedback can be painful but that is how we grow. That's the price of leadership

While I could write volumes on the subject of leadership, one of the most practical powerful ways to demonstrate leadership is via a quality, two-way weekly staff meeting. How else do you get feedback, communicate or build teamwork?

On the following pages, I am providing you with two very useful Leadership tools.

The first is a "Model Staff/Team Meeting" Agenda. The key with anything is to adapt, not adopt other people's good ideas, so feel free to modify as you feel appropriate.

The second document is a "Meeting Evaluation Form" which will allow you to refine and continually improve the quality of your meetings.

In closing, I recommend you consistently hold quality, regular, two-way meetings and use the Semi-Annual Leadership Empowerment Satisfaction Survey to assess your own present effectiveness as a leader.

A MODEL STAFF/ TEAM MEETING - AGENDA

Day: _____   Date: _____

Begin Time: _____   End Time: _____   Location: _____

Personal Action Notes		Item
	1.	Call to order-_____
	2.	Good News Each team member shares best good news, personal or career, since previous meeting.
	3.	Appoint Meeting Recorder
	4.	Business Arising From Minutes • Minutes are reviewed with the objective of ensuring that previous team decisions were effectively followed up.
	5.	Administration Report • Team leader briefs everyone on activities, as well as decisions resulting from most recent Executive/Administrator Meeting.
	6.	Personal Progress Reports • Each team member has the opportunity to brief peers on activities and/ or issues of concern.
	7.	New Business: 1. _____ 2. _____ 3 _____
	8.	Meeting Summary • Meeting chair summarizes key decisions taken and commitments made.
	9.	Calendar Announcements • Review upcoming meetings / events, education opportunities.
	10.	Meeting Evaluation • Everyone completes meeting evaluation form.
	11.	Next Staff / Team Meeting Day:_____Date:_____ Location:_____ Time From: _____ To: _____
	12.	Good of the Team Each team member shares their best idea gained from the meeting, or any comment, suggestion or criticism (along with a positive solution) in the best interest of the group.
	13.	Adjourn!

MEETING EVALUATION FORM

Please Print Clearly:

You've just heard from us, now we'd like to hear from you. Evaluation is the "Breakfast of Champions" - and a critical part of our goal of continuously improving customer satisfaction. Thank you for your help.

Facilitator/Chair Name: _____   Date: _____

My First Name: _____   Last Name: _____

Department: _____   Position: _____

1. What I liked best about this meeting was:

    _____

    _____

2. Recommendation on how the meeting and/or the Just D.O. I.T. process could be improved:

    _____

    _____

3. Constructive feedback for the facilitator:

    _____

    _____

4. I rate the value of my participation in this meeting as:
    (Excellent)   5   4   3   2   1   (Poor)

5. I rate the overall value of this meeting as:
    (Excellent)   5   4   3   2   1   (Poor)

6. The one area I am going to work most on between this and the next meeting is:

    _____

    _____

P.S.

    _____

    _____

Chapter Twenty-Five

EMPATHY

*"There's something about that person that
I just can't stand about me."*
Old Psychology Saying

*"The majority of human beings are more
alike than we are unlike."*
Maya Angelou

Early on in my career, I was asked to speak at a roast for my colleague, a member of city council. We shared an office.

Like everything else in those days, I was in a rush. So the day of the roast I bought a joke book at a bookstore, then went to the hotel early thinking I would prepare at the last minute. No problem! Well the hotel had just opened the bar, thank goodness. It was a hot day in May and I immediately consumed three gin and tonics. I was thirsty. But no problem because it just relaxes you. By now, guests were arriving and I was having a great time. It was happy hour. During the next hour and a half

I had a great time greeting friends while consuming another half dozen cocktails, but no problem because it just relaxes you!

It was now time to begin and the M.C. had arranged for the roasts to be seated at sub-head tables in groups of four. There were two bottles of wine at each sub-head table. One red, one white. I shrewdly noticed the other three roasters were drinking the white, so being the thrifty kind of guy that I am, I drank the red. All of it. 'But no problem because it just relaxes you'. I proceeded to finish preparing my notes.

Would you like to know who was there? The Who's Who of Calgary. The mayor, city council, members of the legislature, the press, fundraisers, everyone who was anyone was there.

The first two speakers were brilliant. The third speaker was the former mayor, Rod Sykes, and he was great.

It was now my turn to speak. I couldn't even read my notes. The first thing I did was tell the same joke the previous speaker had just told. Except he remembered the punch line and I'll be damned if I could. Someone in the audience yelled, "Get a hook." Everyone laughed and I thought that they were laughing with me. They were laughing at me.

The chairman tapped me on the shoulder and said, "Brian, I think you are done." No, I am not. I have a question for you. Have you ever woken up the morning after, not only experiencing the worst hangover of your life, but with the realization that your career had just evaporated the night before? In fact, you didn't want to get out of bed for the rest of your life, but your mother made you!

Now I did everything I could do to avoid going down to city hall, hoping that nobody was talking about it. Everybody was talking about it. I would change the subject and they would change it back.

Now I am telling you this story because this is the opening story I share when I train our new customer service trainers on how to train (we ask their Service Excellence Advisors). So why would I share this story at the beginning of a two-day course, which may be one of the most nerve-wracking educational experiences for them in their life? Why would I tell it? To show them I am human and that I make mistakes. Is it possible they too are about to make mistakes? And what happened when I made the mistake? I messed up, I lived, and I survived. They must too.

When your people make mistakes while getting comfortable with empowerment, or just do dumb things, empathize through self-disclosure. Please write that down. Your people are going to make mistakes, so share with them a little bit of you, when you messed up. What does that achieve? Why don't you make some more notes here.

Number one, it shows you are human.

Number two, they can identify with you. That is important.

Number three, the humor is a release valve.

Number four, you survived; so might they.

Number five, you can teach them how to learn from their mistakes, and

Number six, I have got to ask you a question. Are they now going to be open to advice from you? Yes or no? Yes. Would they necessarily be open to your advice if you didn't do this? Maybe not.

If the situation is a function of performance, then focus upon training.

If they made a mistake because they didn't know any better, you have got to make sure they have the skills they need.

If the situation is a function of poor work habits, then focus upon discipline. If that happens again, we are going to have to take a serious look at your results. Because if you do not give feedback about negative behavior, you sanction incompetence.

Seek and give frequent feedback, otherwise people will think that you've just been to Brian Lee's latest e-seminar. They all have built in skunk detectors, they know when they are being are being techniqued.

Here's a useful tool you can use to apply what you've learned. It's called "One Mistake I'll Never Make Again."

What was the mistake? I got drunk before I spoke.

Why did it happen? I didn't know any better. I thought you were supposed to have a drink before you spoke. Didn't you? That's what everybody told me.

What did I do to fix or minimize the damage? Nothing. There was absolutely nothing I could do there. Nothing was salvageable, I'm afraid.

What did I do so that it will never happen again? I don't drink before I speak. For sure, I didn't stop at the bar on my way to record the e-seminar. There was one exception however. My wedding day. I was actually drinking diet coke at the banquet head table when I turned to my wife and noticed that she was putting back a double rum and coke. So I said what the heck, I'm going to take my chances. Now I have seen the video of the evening and everything seemed to be okay.

What other mistakes in waiting can I fix, or what other opportunities can I take advantage of? That disaster caused me to get serious about speaking, because I love speaking. I had been humiliated and made out to be a fool at something that was so important to me. I decided to treat every future speaking opportunity as if it was my first or my last. I resolved that every time I spoke I was going to improve by 1%. It ended up being a painful but marvelous learning opportunity, but it took me a long time to acknowledge it. I was so embarrassed I avoided telling the story for three years, and only then, out of town.

Russell Ewing once said, "The new leader is clearly distinguished from the old style boss. A boss creates fear; a leader creates confidence. A boss fixes blame, a leader corrects mistakes." And I think that you are going to find self-disclosure a useful way to correct mistakes.

In this chapter you have learned that, when staff make mistakes, both they and you can learn invaluable lessons to grow and mature and continually improve as a result.

To close, let me summarize a few action recommendations.

1. Instead of being critical of your employee or ignoring the problem, empathize with them. Let them know you understand their difficulty and frustration.

2. Through "self-disclosure", share with your employee a similar situation that demonstrates you really do understand how they might feel.

3. If they messed up because they were not educated properly, or didn't know any better, then make sure you fix that training gap.

4. On the other hand, if the foul-up was the result of poor work habits, then you need to take the appropriate disciplinary steps.

5. Above all, be sure to coach them by both of you completing together the "One Mistake I'll Never Make Again" form.

One Mistake I'll Never Make Again

1. What the mistake was: (describe actual event)

    _____

    _____

    _____

    _____

2. Why it happened: (I forgot, someone let me down, etc.)

    _____

    _____

    _____

    _____

    _____

3. What I did to fix it or minimize the damage: (what's salvageable, what's the opportunity)

_____

_____

_____

_____

4. What I did so it would never happen again: (set up file, got educated, changed the system, etc.)

_____

_____

_____

_____

5. What other mistakes-in-writing can I fix, or what opportunities can I take advantage of because of this lesson?

_____

_____

_____

_____

_____

Chapter Twenty-Six

HAVING FUN

*"You can learn more about a person in one hour
of play than a lifetime of conversation."*
Plato

The City was Buffalo, New York. My clients were 300 nurse professionals employed by Visiting Nurses of America.

One of the nursing teams was a totally dysfunctional group who could barely stand working with each other.

At the start of this 12-week Service Excellence process, we announced that as part of their team building exercise they were to party together at least once.

They chose laser tag. Have you ever played laser tag? I know of no other game that can instantly cause adults to revert to childhood. The joy of killing someone and doing it as a team. The agony of defeat.

The impact on the team was dramatic. They bonded! Besides improving employee relations, does anyone have any doubt about the positive impact this change had on their customer service and over all productivity?

A hospital housekeeping department that worked the early shift surprised the late shift with a potluck dinner. The late shift responded with their own surprise meal for their new buddies. At our Service Excellence graduation "Brag Fair", an AM shift team member proudly said, "We used to be co-workers, now we're friends."

Constructive Socializing keeps people together. Schedule some playtime for your staff. Friday night beer busts, potluck parties, a night on the town, bowling, anything that will get people laughing and playing together. After all, a team that plays together, and hugs together, stays together.

Recommendation: Schedule creative quarterly appropriate social opportunities to break down barriers and give permission to have fun.

> *"Loyalty at work hasn't come to an end...*
> *It's been replaced with loyalty to one's friends."*
> Brian Lee CSP

P =

Physician

Acceptance

Chapter Twenty-Seven

WHAT NURSES WOULD CHANGE

"Healthcare's dirty little secret is the pathetic way doctors treat nurses."
Anonymous

When it comes to the issues of nurse retention and employee morale, are physicians part of the solution or are they part of the problem?

To put this issue in perspective I want to share with you a dozen typical comments originating from Nurse Focus Groups prior to the launch of our "Physician Service Excellence" process in Hospitals.

Please proceed with empathy;

- "I can't count the number of times I've cried. If you do, they'll take advantage."

- "In my wildest dream, I could not imagine asking a doctor to help me."

- New nurse grads need to be taught they don't need to begin every conversation with, "I'm sorry."

- "We spend way too much time teaching new staff not to take rude behavior personally."
- "Doctors seem to think they're God and everybody else is a nobody. There's no respect."
- They lack social graces. They treat us like a piece of furniture. We're not in their social strata."
- "Our poor orderlies get beat up."
- "We often feel devalued. They'll put their chart right on top of the one I'm already working on."
- "When a new doctor is pleasant...give 'em six months!"
- "We're the patient advocate. They don't see us that way."
- "It's like we're invisible. I can spend a great deal of time helping a doctor and get zero acknowledgement."
- "Peer review is not effective. It just doesn't work."

This is typical feedback from nurses about doctors and it's a subject matter that I feel very strongly about.

I should clarify that not all doctors are guilty of these behaviors, but too many are.

Rather than encouraging nurses to be assertive and respond to unnecessary rudeness with "that behavior is unacceptable", the nursing profession traditionally teaches them to, "not take it personally." After years of consistent discourtesy and indifference to you as a person, how can you not?

Unless there is an empathic / medical visionary Chief of Staff, peer review doesn't work because doctors will not hold each other accountable. It's bad for referrals.

This subject disappoints me. Like everyone else, I believed doctors were special people who were committed to making a difference ...until I learned how they treat their staff.

Yes, there are exceptions. And there are some nurses with good self-esteem who refuse to be walked over. However there are way too many horror stories than we'd like to admit.

Chapter Twenty-Eight

SUCCESSFULLY INVOLVING PHYSICIANS

It's critical to involve physicians in your staff retention process because they need to be part of the solution. Patients see them as part of the same team. The irony is that the doctors who are the angriest about the quality of nursing not being what it used to be are the ones driving nurses away.

During the past two years we have been working with hospitals to successfully involve physicians to improve Service Excellence, employee morale and retention.

Here are my recommendations to successfully involve doctors in your nurse retention Service Excellence process.

1. Involve Your Chief of Staff.

Involve your Chief of Staff right at the beginning. Sit down and discuss the problem and ask him or her for a commitment.

2.   Conduct a Nurse Focus Group

Use an outsider to conduct a nurse focus group.

Ask attendees, including LVN's and other primary support staff:

1. What do you like best about working with the physicians here? The answers won't take very long.

2. If you could change three things about your working relationship with doctors, with the goal of improving communication, patient satisfaction and employee morale and retention, what would they be?

3. What do you need to do to personally improve this situation?

3.   Share the results with all your doctors

Share the results of the focus group with your doctors. I did exactly this for a Southern California Hospital with about 300 doctors in attendance. I also shared positive educational ideas to help them build their Physician Practice along with the results of a staff focus group. You could hear a pin drop. The organizers wondered if attendees might walk out on me but nobody left. Do you know why? The information was relevant and I suspect few had any idea they and their colleagues were perceived so negatively.

4.   Adopt a Physician Empowerment Policy.

A policy designed to address physician/nurse issues that relate to courtesy, communication, chart clarity, peer communication, telephone courtesy, on-call colleagues, nurse-patient co-advocacy, and more.

If you want your doctors to own this policy, they need to become involved in the authoring it. There must be standards of mutual self-respect. Invite doctors to sign off on the final document. This could become a pre-requisite factor for renewing a doctor's hospital admitting privileges. For a sample policy see Chapter #29

5. Implement a (voluntary) semi-annual Physician Empowerment Survey.

This concept is modeled on the Leadership Empowerment Survey you learned about in Chapter #14. Implement a semi-annual Physician Empowerment Survey that reflects both the content of this policy and measure its effectiveness.

To begin with, invite your doctors to sign up for it on a voluntary basis. The nurse director would administer the survey in the units where doctors are frequent and active.

For sample survey see Chapter #30.

6. Make sure your "incident form" has a place to check off "Professional Misconduct."

7. Peer Review Reform

If necessary, reform your Physician peer review process with the consent and involvement of your medical leadership.

8. Nurse Assertiveness Communication Training.

Offer assertiveness communication training for nurses. I don't understand why it's not being offered in nursing schools now.

9. Encourage department based Nurse/Physician Socials

Schedule parties together. Again, let me quote Plato, "You can learn more about a person in one hour of play than a lifetime of conversation."

10. Provide Joint Physician – Nurse Communication Training.

For this you will need encouragement and support from Administrators and your Chief Medical Officer.

11. Provide Physicians (and their staff) with Service Excellence Training.

The focus with Doctors should be on empowerment similar in content to this book.

This process provides tools but they won't cure all ills. However, it does offer you a proven strategy and maybe it's time to address the secret that is really not much of a secret.

In the remaining pages of this chapter, I have supplied a flowchart that reflects this process.

Physician Education / Involvement Strategies
The Service Excellence Initiative

This Flowchart Depicts the 7 optional Physician Education /
Involvement training and implementation programs

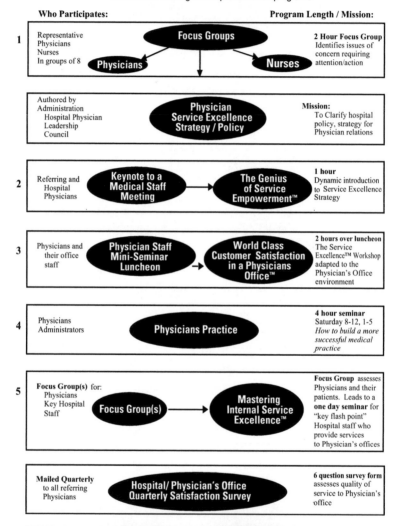

Who Participates: **Program Length / Mission:**

1
Representative
Physicians
Nurses
In groups of 8

Focus Groups
Physicians — Nurses

2 Hour Focus Group
Identifies issues of
concern requiring
attention/action

Authored by
Administration
 Hospital Physician
 Leadership
 Council

Physician
Service Excellence
Strategy / Policy

Mission:
To Clarify hospital
policy, strategy for
Physician relations

2
Referring and
Hospital
Physicians

Keynote to a
Medical Staff
Meeting
The Genius
of Service
Empowerment™

1 hour
Dynamic introduction
to Service Excellence
Strategy

3
Physicians and
their office
staff

Physician Staff
Mini-Seminar
Luncheon
World Class
Customer Satisfaction
in a Physicians
Office™

2 hours over luncheon
The Service
Excellence™ Workshop
adapted to the
Physician's Office
environment

4
Physicians
Administrators

Physicians Practice

4 hour seminar
Saturday 8-12, 1-5
*How to build a more
successful medical
practice*

5
Focus Group(s) for:
Physicians
Key Hospital
Staff

Focus Group(s)
Mastering
Internal Service
Excellence™

Focus Group assesses
Physicians and their
patients. Leads to a
one day seminar for
"key flash point"
Hospital staff who
provide services
to Physician's offices

Mailed Quarterly
to all referring
Physicians

Hospital/ Physician's Office
Quarterly Satisfaction Survey

6 question survey form
assesses quality of
service to Physician's
office

6
Physicians Office
Staff
Key Hospital
Service
Providers

Medical Office
Assistant Professional
Association
Medical Office
Assistant Hospital
Professional Certificate
Program

Continuous on-campus
education for medical
assistants, with
certificate recognition
program

Solving Unit Specific / Low Physician Scores
The Service Excellence Initiative (cont'd)

Who Participates: **Program Length / Mission:**

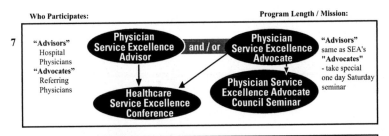

7 "Advisors"
   Hospital
   Physicians
   "Advocates"
   Referring
   Physicians

   "Advisors"
   same as SEA's
   "Advocates"
   - take special
   one day Saturday
   seminar

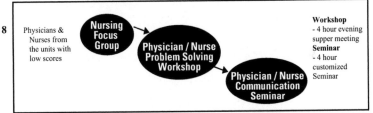

8 Physicians &
   Nurses from
   the units with
   low scores

   Workshop
   - 4 hour evening
   supper meeting
   Seminar
   - 4 hour
   customized
   Seminar

Physician Staff - Mini Seminar Luncheon Series

9 Physician Office
   Staff

   2 hour
   seminar with
   buffet lunch

Focus Group(s) with
Nurses, Patients

1 day seminar
Key communication
skills of critical core
competencies

Chapter Twenty-Nine

PHYSICIAN SERVICE EMPOWERMENT POLICY™

PHYSICIAN SERVICE EMPOWERMENT POLICY™

17 Attributes of a Successful Professional Physician/Hospital Staff Relationship

Physician Name (Please Print)_____

A. Creating a Culture of World Class Customer Satisfaction

To assist *(Hospital Name)* physicians and staff to create a truly patient driven culture of world class Customer Satisfaction, *(Hospital Name)* Medical Staff leadership has developed the following "Attributes of a Successful Professional Physician/ Hospital Staff Relationship" as a positive guideline to reinforce its commitment to "Principles of Partnership."

B. We Need Your Help

We ask all *(Hospital Name)* physicians and hospital staff to help make these attributes a part of our everyday culture. Would you please review the Service Excellence policy statement and indicate your agreement with your signature on the last page.

C. The Service Excellence Initiative

To facilitate these objectives we are undertaking a series of ongoing professional development initiatives that will further these goals, as part of our organization-wide initiative of Service Excellence.

D. At *(Hospital Name)*, **physicians, hospital staff and other practitioners exercising clinical privileges in the Hospital will:**

1. **Demonstrate courtesy/respect.**

    1.1 Begin every contact with a courteous greeting including calling staff by name.

    1.2 Speak directly to each other, establishing eye contact and using a positive tone of voice and body language.

    1.3 At all times, show all (Hospital Name)staff personnel respect and courtesy, avoiding:

    • Yelling or use of profane or vulgar language
    • Intimidating or degrading comments
    • Racial, ethnic, religious, or sexual references
    • Making any negative personal references in front of anyone else
    • Expecting staff to get you coffee, meal orders, or take your personal calls

    1.4 Treat auxiliary and support staff with the same standards enumerated here with nurses.

2. **Patient/ Family Communication**

    2.1 Anticipate patient and family questions about treatment, especially potential adverse reaction to prescriptions. Nursing staff will make every effort to coordinate physician meeting time with the family to maximize efficiency of time.

2.2 Whenever possible, the attending/primary physician should talk directly to family members and answer their questions.

2.3 Give the patient your undivided attention, and make every effort to ensure they really understand what they're being told, i.e., sit on a chair and make eye-to-eye contact with the patient.

2.4 Never share concerns about nursing or the hospital with the patient or family (hearing this hurts the patient rather than helps them). Sharing of problems should be done in private.

2.5 Refrain from any negative reference whatsoever in front of the patient and family about staff, the hospital and colleagues.

2.6 Do encourage patients to share their concerns with you, the nurse, or management.

2.7 With critical care patients involving multiple physicians, the primary attending doctor should make an effort to coordinate communication with the patient and family.

3. Physician Orders

3.1 Make every effort to brief nursing staff on the condition of the patient by:

- Inviting them into the room during patient assessment, and/or

- Speaking to them directly about the plan of care prior to departure, and

- answer any questions they may have about treatment.

3.2 Ensure nurse is fully conversant with the Patient Plan of Care, including all relevant remarks made directly to the patient.

3.3 Wherever possible, issue standing orders or Clinical Pathways for use of Tylenol, Maalox, etc.

3.4 It is a physician's responsibility to explain the risks, benefits, and alternative treatments in order to obtain an informed consent. A nurse may only be asked to obtain the signature.

3.5 Give physician orders that can be clearly understood.

3.6 Provide, as appropriate, a written diagnosis for all out-patient orders/treatment (Medicare requirement).

4. Chart Clarity

4.1 Use legible handwriting or print neatly and review written orders directly with the nurse.

4.2 Strongly consider printing your hospital number below (beside) your signature, or print your name, if live contact with the nurse is not possible.

5. Peer Communication

5.1 Take responsibility for designating a "Captain of the Ship" to avoid confusion where multiple physicians are involved.

5.2 Ensure the admitting or attending doctor takes responsibility for contacting and communicating with consulting physicians ("Captain of the Ship").

5.3 Avoid criticizing each other in front of staff or patients and family members.

5.4 Take responsibility for reading each other's progress notes and orders.

5.6 Take responsibility for holding each other accountable for respectful professional conduct.

6. Telephone/ Courtesy

6.1 Return calls in a timely, prompt way.

6.2 Begin the call with a friendly greeting and conclude it with a polite good-bye (remember, they are calling you about your patient).

6.3 Refrain from use of the instruction "I don't want to be called anymore" or "Don't call me, especially with ABNORMALS, or about patient pain."

7. Office Liason

7.1 Avoid voice mail systems that do not facilitate timely direct human access to hospital personnel. There needs to be a mechanism to recognize an "urgent" call.

7.2 Ensure office staff makes every effort to locate you, upon request.

7.3 Ensure telephone exchange personnel respond in a timely and helpful manner.

8. On-Call Colleagues

8.1 Takes responsibility that on-call colleagues are fully briefed on patient's condition, especially on weekends and holidays.

9. Discharge Planning

9.1 Make every effort to provide clear advance directives, nutritional, and discharge orders.

10. Teacher/ Mentor

10.1 Show discretion in service expectations from the various levels of medical certification (RN, LVN) and practical experience (vs. new graduate).

10.2 Respect staff's ability to prioritize conflicting patient/physician requests.

10.3 Be understanding of the unique and difficult challenges faced by night shift personnel.

11. Nurse Patient Co-advocacy

11.1 Fully appreciate and respect the nurse's role as patient co-advocate.

11.2 Respect the nurse's need to speak up for herself/ himself when confronted with disruptive behavior.

11.3 When in doubt, give the benefit of the doubt.

11.4 In no way discourage nurses from providing up-to-date information about the patient's medical condition.

11.5 When present and where appropriate, assist the nurse with difficult patient treatments.

11.6 Remember that while staff endeavor to adapt to your personal practice style, they do deal with a multiple of your peers, and patience is required.

12. Compliance

12.5 Recognize and cooperate with the nurse's professional mandated role in adhering to regulatory and medical staff compliance directives.

13. Recognition

13.1 Show appreciation for service provided above and beyond the call of duty.

13.2 Seek opportunities to create and enhance quality professional relationships through personal rapport and social exchanges.

14. Culture

14.1 Recognize (Hospital Name)'s desire to create a patient-driven, physician-supportive, employee-friendly culture that acknowledges everyone's legitimate needs and rights.

15. Principles of Partnership

15.1 Be aware of and adhere to the Medical Staff's peer review policy and expectations.

16. Physician Service Empowerment Survey

16.1 (Hospital Name) staff physicians are encouraged to participate in the Semi-Annual Service Empowerment Survey as a means of being in alignment with this policy.

Reciprocal Note:

It is understood that these standards are applicable equally to all personnel.

Acceptance:

I accept and agree to adhere to the policy and standards set out in this document.

_____

Signature   Date

_____

Please print your name

Chapter Thirty

SEMI-ANNUAL
PHYSICIAN EMPOWERMENT
SATISFACTION SURVEY™

Confidential   Page 1 of 4

Physician Name: _____
Date: _____ 20_____

To assist your leadership team in its mission of creating a "customer-driven culture through people empowerment," we sincerely appreciate your completion of this confidential survey and forwarding it to your Department Director within 48 hours. PLEASE DO NOT IDENTIFY YOURSELF IN ANY WAY. Thank you.

5 – Always   4 – Usually   3 – Sometimes   2 – On Occasion
1 – Never   NA – Not applicable

The physician I work with:

---

1. Courtesy / Respect   5 4 3 2 1 NA

Greets me in a professional and courteous manner and at all times and uses my name.

2. Patient / Family Communication   5 4 3 2 1 NA

Is responsive to patient / family information and empathy needs and effectively answers their questions as to treatment, especially potential adverse reactions.

3. Physician Orders   5 4 3 2 1 NA

Seeks input from and updates me effectively about the patient's condition and plan of care and provides clear physician orders and answers my questions clearly prior to departure.

4. Chart Clarity   5 4 3 2 1 NA

Consistently writes legibly on patient's charts and insures complete and accurate documentation.

5. Peer Communication   5 4 3 2 1 NA

Communicates effectively with peers and is helpful in clarifying who is "Captain of the Ship" where multiple physicians are involved

6. Telephone Courtesy   5 4 3 2 1 NA

Responds to my phone calls in a timely manner and exhibits polite telephone courtesy.

7. Office Liaison
5 4 3 2 1 NA

Insures their office staff or answering service are conveniently accessible by phone and helpful with our requests for assistance

8. On-Call Colleagues
5 4 3 2 1 NA

Takes responsibility that on call colleagues are adequately briefed on patient condition, especially on weekends and holidays.

9. Discharge Planning
5 4 3 2 1 NA

Plans ahead and gives clear discharge directions.

10. Teacher / Mentor
5 4 3 2 1 NA

Demonstrates his/her awareness of the varying levels of licensure, certification, and/or experience, and makes an effort to teach and mentor to me.

11. Nurse Patient Co-Advocacy
5 4 3 2 1 NA

Accepts the nurse's role as patient co-advocate and respects staff's right to speak up when confronted with disruptive behavior.

12. Compliance
5 4 3 2 1 NA

Recognizes and cooperates with nurses' professional mandated role in adhering to regulatory and medical staff compliance directives.

13. Recognition
5 4 3 2 1 NA

Shows appreciation for service provided above and beyond the call of duty.

14. OVERALL, I rate my satisfaction   5   4   3   2   1   NA
with the quality of this professional
relationship as:

PS   I look forward to working   5   4   3   2   1   NA
with him/her.

Please insert into Confidential Envelope and return to the
Department Director within 48 hours.

Chapter Thirty-One

D.O. I.T.

ACTION PLAN

Now that you're finished the book, it's time to D.O. I.T.

D.O. I.T. is an acronym I use in all of our training programs that stands for Daily Ongoing Implementation Tactics

This D.O. I.T. Action plan will assist you in tracking your progress and help your team achieve their goals.

My challenge for you is to earn 6,000 points towards a "Center of Nursing Excellence" designation. If you are successful, we will award your organization a "Center of Nursing Excellence" Certificate.

While this recognition carries no formal sanctioning, it will provide your team with an external acknowledgement of your progress creating a nurse-friendly, customer-driven culture.

First determine which goals you

> Must Do
>
> Should Do
>
> Might Do

Prioritize the "Must Do" goals and rate each of them on a scale of 1-10 with 10 being high and one being low. Then you need to set specific time frames.

Should you require any further clarification or guidance, I can be reached at:

1-800-667-7325; Fax: 403-228-6776; or Email: info@custom-learning.com

P. S. The Nurse Magnet Program

Should you wish to proceed further and explore the option of becoming a "Nurse Magnet" hospital, I have included information in "Addenda A" for your convenience.

THE NURSE RETENTION D.O. I.T.
(Daily Ongoing Implementation Tactics)

Keep Your Nurses & HealthCare Professionals for Life™

Dear Reader/Course Graduate:

Your "D.O.I.T." Action plan has been designed by assigning appropriate "points" for specific actions to assist you to track your progress, and achieve your goals.

My challenge for you is to earn a minimum of 6,000 points, and confirmed by an external auditor of your choice, for which we will award your organization a "Center of Nursing Excellence" Certificate.

The attached "D.O. I.T." Meeting Agenda on the next page is provided for you and your peers to debrief what you have learned form the book and/or seminar.

Feel free to give me a call should you have any questions or special requests at:

- 1-800-667-7325
- Fax: 403-228-6776
- Email: brian@customlearning.com

Brian Lee CSP Founder

P.S. In order to maintain a sense of momentum and enthusiasm and avoid a feeling of being overwhelmed:

1. Determine which goals are:

   A "Must Do"

   B "Should Do"

   C "Might Do"

2. Of the "must do", prioritize by rating each on a scale of 1-10 (10 high, 1 low)

3. Set specific time frames.

"D.O. I.T." (ACT WITH URGENCY) MEETING

Day: _____ Date: _____

Time: From: _____ to _____ Location: _____

1. Call to order by _____

2. Minutes to be taken by: _____

3. Each delegate - shares their recommended implementation strategy in terms of:

   A) "Big Picture" process goals

   B) Utilization of the Just "D.O. I.T." Process

4. Discuss and Develop a Group Consensus on

   A) Big picture - goals

   B) Process for gaining a buy in from:

      1. Key senior decision makers not present,

      2. The entire leadership team.

5. Nurse Retention Team

   A) Does your current team meet the needs of your current strategy

   B. If not   1) Should it be structured/reorganized?

                   2) How and when should that happen?

6. What are the immediate "Next Steps" and who will do what

7. Other Business Arising

   a)_____

   b)_____

   c)_____

8. Our next meeting is to be:

   Day: _____ Date: _____ Time: From: _____ to _____

9. Good of the Group

   Any final comment, idea or suggestion in the best interest of this group.

10. Adjourn

THE EMPOWERED LEADERS JUST D.O. I.T. ACTION PLAN

#	Recommendation (Chapter #)	Points Available	Admin Initial
	**Leader Just D.O. I.T. – Empowerment Action Plan**		
	IMPLEMENTATION STRATEGY		
1.	**Debrief Immediately** Within the next 48 hours, hold a Post "Keep Your Nurses & HealthCare Professionals for Life™" D.O. I.T." (Act With Urgency) Meeting utilizing the agenda provided.	200	
2.	**Commit to a Timeline** "Make a Commitment, Keep Your Commitment!" by setting a timeline for these goals.	200	
3.	**Strategize a "Buy in"** Develop a consensus "sales strategy" to gain a buy in from your key decision makers	200	
4.	**Executive Briefing** Conduct an "Executive Briefing" for the entire management team in which you: 1. Share the results of this seminar & your research 2. Propose your solution/strategy- with dates 3. Answer questions 4. Ask for a commitment	500	
5.	**Nurse Retention Council** 1. Appoint (or reorganize an existing team) a "Nurse Retention" Council 2. Representative of your entire organization 3. 50% management/50% front line 4. Lead and "sponsored" by a your CNE 5. With a clear written council charter • mandate • mission • time frame • budget • authority to plan, communicate and implement	500	

D.O. I.T. Action Plan

	Leader Just D.O. I.T. – Empowerment Action Plan		
#	Recommendation (Chapter #)	Points Available	Admin Initial
	IMPLEMENTATION STRATEGY		
6.	Make nurse retention priority #1 & appoint a C.R.O. ("Chief Retention Officer")	200	
7.	Designate every Nurse Leader as a "Nurse Retention Officer" and offer recognition and incentives.	200	
8.	Appoint a "Nurse Retention Project Team"	200	
9.	Ask everyone: 1. "If you were going to leave...What would be your #1 peeve?" 2. "Do you reserve the right to change your mind?" 3. "What would cause you to change your mind?"	200	
10.	Daily Excellence Diary. Maintain a daily Excellence Diary for 21 days recording ideas, skills, improvements, or systems that you either learn about or actually implement each day.	100	
	IMPERATIVE #1 – K = THE KEY IS CULTURE		
11.	Conduct an assessment of your current culture and share it with everyone. Utilize input from everyone to identify your actual culture, brainstorm your preferred culture.	200	
12.	Hold your management accountable for creating an empowering departmental culture. Ask for quarterly progress reports.	200	
	IMPERATIVE #2 — E = EMPOWERMENT IS THE WAY		
13.	Implement a "Service Recovery Policy" to implement "The Complaint Golden Rule": "Mess Up, Fess Up, Dress Up!" - Brian Lee CSP	200	
14.	Non-Productive Staff Removal. Successfully, legally and effectively remove chronically non-productive staff	200	
15.	Implement a dynamic, grass roots recognition & appreciation process. Use the "My L.I.S.T." Tool.	200	
16.	Make everyone an insider by agreeing upon 3 critical numbers that everyone should know and make sure that they know.	100	
17.	Show empathy by M.B.W.A. (Manage By Walking Around) 15% of your time	100	

IMPERATIVE #2 — E = EMPOWERMENT IS THE WAY (cont'd)		
18.	**Front Line "Sabbatical"** Serve in a front line position one day every three months (unless doing more already). (Counts points only if this is a change in your role.)	200 per day
19.	**Service Recovery Policy** In close consultation with your front line, draft the policy for and implement a Service Recovery Fund to apply "Mess Up, Fess Up and Dress Up"	500
20.	Invest one hour of active listening with every direct report.	500
21.	Schedule quality, 2 way, weekly staff meetings.	500
22.	Organize a cool staff social at least once every quarter.	200
IMPERATIVE #3 — E = EDUCATION & ENGAGEMENT		
23.	Give your people a cause that captivates the imagination and stirs the soul and "Focus on Patient Care" by consulting with every one to adopt a department based patient satisfaction measurement goal.	200
24.	**Make the front line accountable for teaching Customer Satisfaction** Recruit the "Best of the Best" Front Line stars and train them to teach customer satisfaction and serve as a peer role model for a 1 year term. We call them: "Service Excellence Advisors"	500
25.	Create a mentoring program.	200
26.	**Annual Education Plan** Develop an annual departmental/unit continuous education plan.	200
27.	**Leadership Empowerment Satisfaction Survey** 1. The "Leadership Empowerment Satisfaction Survey" should be conducted 2 times per year. 2. You are to conduct your second survey and receive the results no later than one week prior to the "Service Summit" 3. Please note the following survey categories: (Question #9, Overall) Category Overall Rating A 4.5 – 5 B 4.0 - 4.49 C 3.5 - 3.99 D 3.0 - 3.49 E less than 3.0 4. You will receive 500 points per category improvement, i.e. • move from B to A = 500 points • move from D to B = 1000 points 5. If you are already in category A, you receive 250 points for staying in that same category	500 points per category

D.O. I.T. Action Plan

Leader Just D.O. I.T. – Empowerment Action Plan			
#	Recommendation (Chapter #)	Points Available	Admin Initial
IMPERATIVE #4 — P = PHYSICIAN ACCEPTANCE			
28.	Involve your Chief of Staff in your nurse retention and patient satisfaction process.	200	
29.	Conduct a Nurse Focus Group. 200 30. Share the results with all your Doctors.	200	
31.	Adopt a Physician Empowerment Policy. (See toolkit)	200	
32.	Implement a (voluntary) semi-annual Physician Empowerment Survey. (See toolkit)	200	
33.	Offer Nurse Assertiveness Communication training.	200	
34.	Provide joint Physician - Nurse Communication Training.	200	
35.	Provide Physicians (& their staff) with Service Excellence Training	100	
ACCOUNTABILITY			
36.	Do a Cost Analysis of retention versus turnover costs Note: Consider a training Goal of 3.5% of budget = $1500 a year - Retention • Calculate the real cost of recruitment/ replacement	200	
37.	Performance Review Incentive Adopt a management bonus program to incentivize leadership based upon nurse retention rates.	200	
38.	Conduct "exit interviews" with every single departing nurse and utilize results for continuous improvement.	200	
GOAL SETTING SUMMARY			
A.	Total Points Available 9300	9300	
B.	My / Our Goal		
C.	Required to receive Custom Learning Systems Group Ltd. designation "Nurse Magnet" Facility. 6000	6000	

Nurse Retention "D.O. I.T." Bragg Memo

Date: _____

To: **Nurse Retention Registrar**

Custom Learning Systems Group Ltd.

Phone: 245-2428 Fax: 228-6776

Email: info@customlearning.com

RE: YES! WE DID IT!

As you can see from the attached documentation and initialed "D.O. I.T." Action Plan, we have successful attained a minimum of 6,000 points in the process of implementing a culture change to improve nurse retention.

Please forward to us ASAP our "Center of Nursing Excellence." Thank you.

NAME: _____ POSITION: _____

ORGANIZATION: _____

DEPARTMENT: _____

BUSINESS ADDRESS: _____

CITY: _____ PROV./STATE: _____ PC/ZIP: _____

BUS PHONE: (_____)_____ FAX: (_____)_____

RES: (_____)_____ E-MAIL # _____

Chapter Thirty-Two

MAKE A

COMMITMENT

"If your ship doesn't come in, swim out to it."
Jonathan Winters

One final question, do you believe the strategies and goals of the book are achievable?

Changing your hospital's culture and rooted behaviors must be a concentrated effort from the top down and reverse.

Is the status quo working for you? Will it ensure a dedicated and qualified staff next year or in the year 2020? Don't stick this book in a drawer. Use it as a blueprint. Remember, for every new nurse, four are leaving. If staff losses cost you $75,000 (150%) of the annual compensation plus advertising, orientation, and other related costs equaling a total of $95,000, your bottom line on four nurses is $380,000.

If you can create an environment that encourages people to stay and sell, how much money will you save? More importantly, how much will your people contribute if they feel valued and appreciated and know that you respect them as individuals?

You have a choice. You can be willing to change your culture or be doomed to repeat the past. Is the past working? Is it attracting people to the nursing profession?

These actions begin by doing a 1,000 things one percent better and don't forget to ask everyone:

1. "If you were going to leave, what would be your number one peeve?" And if they reply, "I'm not leaving," keep asking.
2. "Do you reserve the right to change your mind?"
3. "What would cause you to change your mind?"

CONCLUSION

My belief is "Life changes not when we begin to act, but when we commit to act."

Here's a final thought about the importance of commitment . . .

Commitment

Commitment is what transforms a promise into reality

It is the words that speak boldly of your intentions.

And the actions which speak louder than words.

It is making the time when there is none.

Coming through time after time, year after year after year.

Commitment is the stuff that character is made of;

The power to change the face of things.

It is the daily triumph of integrity

Over skepticism.

> **"Make a Commitment,
> Keep Your Commitment!"**

NURSE MAGNET PROGRAM

*"When your life is filled with the desire
to see the holiness in everyday life,
something magical happens: ordinary life
becomes extraordinary and the very process
of life begins to nourish your soul."*
Rabbi Harold Kushner

THE NURSE MAGNET PROGRAM

By implementing a change in your hospital culture to improve nurse retention, you can qualify as a "Center of Nursing Excellence" through Custom Learning Systems Group Ltd.

The Nurse Magnet Program is another form of recognition but by your peers. The following explains the criteria plus the application and appraisal process.

The Magnet Nursing Services Recognition Program is based on the American Nurses Association's Scope and Standards for Nurse Administrators (ANA, 1996, Pub #NS-35). The applicant facility provides documentation and evidence that supports and verifies that they are implementing the standards throughout the nursing service.

An applicant must purchase The Magnet Nursing Services Recognition Program for Excellence in Nursing Services, HealthCare Organization, Instructions and Application Process (ANCC, 2000, Pub #MAGMAN00). It outlines the entire application process and contains the application form plus all the necessary directions for preparing the written documentation. This manual is priced at $50 U.S., plus shipping and handling.

Eligibility Requirements

To be eligible to apply, a healthcare organization must meet the following requirements:

The applicant nursing service system exists within a healthcare organization.

The healthcare organization nursing service includes one or more nursing settings with a single governing authority and one individual serving as the Nurse Administrator.

Scope and Standards for Nurse Administrators (ANA, 1996) are currently being implemented by the nursing system.

In the five years preceding the application, the applicant nursing service must not have committed an unfair labor practice.

Applicants for Magnet recognition are required to participate in ANA's National Database of Nursing Quality Indicators (NDNQI). This project addresses the issues of patient safety and quality of care arising from changes in healthcare delivery.

Magnet Program Information

To order the manual for the Magnet Recognition Program, access order forms online (ANCC@ana.org), or call (800) 637-0323. Include $50 plus shipping and handling.

Please call the Magnet Program Staff at (202) 651-7262 for information about the Magnet Recognition Program. The staff members are:

Executive Director, ANCC

Kammie Monarch, Director of Accreditation and Magnet Recognition Program

Mary Moon Allison, BSN, MH, SE, Magnet Program Specialist

Stephen H. Snell, Magnet Program Specialist, Acute Care

Contact: American Nurses Credentialing Center
Suite 100 West, 600 Maryland Avenue SW
Washington, DC 20024-2571
ANCC@ana.org
ANCC catalogs: 1-800-284-2378

BOOK AT A GLANCE

The Big Picture

1. Time is running out. The average nurse's age is between 42 and 48 and the proportion of nurses under the age of 30 has dropped from 30 percent to 12 percent.

Trends in Healthcare

2. We have to reestablish the agenda back centered on people issues.

The Facts in Nursing Today

3. We need to reduce our costs and improve our outcomes simultaneously.

4. It's expected that within a few years, 1.7 million nurses will be needed in both Canada and the United States.

Why are Nurses Leaving?

5. Healthcare is perceived as a lousy environment.

6. Appoint a Nurse Retention Officer and ask everyone

    a   If you were going to leave, what would be your number one peeve? And if they reply, "I'm not leaving." Ask it again and keep asking until they give you an answer.

    b   Do you reserve the right to change your mind?

    c   What would cause you to change your mind?

7. Get good at hiring right the first time.

Excellence is the Answer

8. The cost of turnover is $95,000 per employee.
9. There is a direct relationship between nurse retention and patient satisfaction.
10. A one percent change in morale equals a two percent change in customer satisfaction.

The Key is Culture

11. Change your culture or be doomed to repeat the past.
12. Conduct an assessment of your current culture and share it with everyone.
13. Utilize everyone to help you define your exact culture and brainstorm your new culture.
14. Hold your management accountable to empower you to create a new culture.
15. Write a vision statement for your new culture.

Empowerment is the Way

16. Trust your people, give them responsibility, grant them the authority and hold them accountable.
17. Employee morale has nothing to do with how hard people work.
18. Value your people as your greatest asset.

Respect

19. Common courtesy shouldn't be so uncommon that it is mistaken for genius.

Communication

20. MBWA: Management by wandering around. Spend 15 percent of your time to stop and say hello to every individual (without an agenda on your part).
21. Listen to your people.

Alignment and Trust

22. The four pillars of trust are acceptance, reliability, openness, and congruence.
23. Keep your agreements because people will remember them.

Recognition and Feedback

24. Give people feedback on the things they do well and the things they don't do well.
25. Recognition is only appreciated if it's a) timely, b) spontaneous, c) specific, and d) geared to that individual.

Empowerment

26. Until your front line owns your customer service problems, you'll never solve your customer service problems.
27. Empower your staff with the Complaint Golden Rule and establish a service recovery fund.

Education and Engagement

28. When your people are learning, they're not leaving.

Insider Information

29. People want to be treated as an insider.

Coach and Champion

30. If you want people to care about what they're doing, you first have to show them that you care about what they want to be.

Mentorship

31. Telling people what they should be doing reminds you that you should practice what you teach.
32. A mentor's role is to teach, guide, counsel and challenge.

Training and Tools

33. People need the tools to do the job.

34. Implement empowerment training.

35. Ask the best of your front line staff to become trainers.

36. The most powerful recruitment program is peers recruiting peers, because they believe in what they're doing.

Leadership

37. Have quality, two-way staff meetings.

38. Use the Semi-Annual Leadership Empowerment Satisfaction Survey to assess your own effectiveness as a leader.

Empathy

39. The most useful thing you can do is emphasize through s e l f -disclosure.

Having Fun

40. Schedule playtime for your staff.

41. A team that plays together and hugs together, stays together.

Physician Acceptance

42. Involve physicians in staff retention.

43. Get an outsider to conduct a nurse focus group and share the results with your physicians.

RECOMMENDED
READING / WEBSITES

Staff Retention

1. Love 'Em or Lose 'Em: Getting Good People to Stay - Beverly L. Kaye, Sharon Jordan-Evans

2. Keeping Good Business People: Strategies for Solving the #1 Problem Facing Businesses Today - Roger E. Herman

3. Overturn Turnover: Why Some Employees Leave, Why Some Employees Stay & Ways to Keep the Ones You Want to Stay - Paul R. Ahr, Thomas B. Ahr

4. Competing for Talent: Key Recruitment and Retention Strategies for Becoming an Employer of Choice - Nancy S. Ahlrichs

5. Keeping the People Who Keep You in Business: 24 Ways to Hang on to Your Most Valuable Talent - F. Leigh Branham

6. The Teenage Worker - Fred Martels, Kathy Pennell

7. Creating Commitment: How to Attract and Retail Talented Employees by Building Relationships That Last - Michael O'Malley

8. Keeping Your Valuable Employees: Retention Strategies for Your Organization's Most Important Resource - Suzanne Dibble

9. Recruit & Retain The Best - Ray Schreyer, John Lewis, Jr. McCarter

10. Harvard Business Review on Finding & Keeping the Best People

11. Managing with Carrots: Using Recognition to Attract and Retain the Best People - Chester Elton & Adrian Robert Gostick

12. 1,001 Ways to Reward Employees - Bob Nelson

Nurse Retention

13. The Nursing Shortage - Nursing World (Jan. 31, 2001) - Brenda Nevidjon, RN, MSN and Jeanette Ives Erikson, RN, MS, CAN

Change Management

14. Leading Change - John Kotter - Harvard Press

RECOMMENDED WEBSITES
DISCUSSING THE NURSING SHORTAGE

American Nurses' Association	http://nursingworld.org
Nurses for a Healthier Tomorrow	http://www.nursesource.org/
Nursing Economics	http://www.ajj.com
The Forum on Healthcare Leadership	http://www.healthcareforum.org
National League of Nursing	http://www.nln.org
Bureau of Labor Statistics	http://www.bls.gov
American Hospital Association	http://www.aha.org
American Organization of Nurse Executives	http://www.aone.org
American Association of Colleges of Nursing	http://aacn.nche.edu
Allnurses.com	http://allnurses.com
Nurse.com	http://nurse.com
HRLive	http://hrlive.com/reports/

Other Websites:

Specific State Nurses' Association

Nursing Specialty Organizations

Source: The Nursing Shortage

Nursing World. Brenda Nevidjon, RN, MSN

Jeanette Ives Erikson, RN, MS, CNA

DIRECTORY OF PROFESSIONAL NURSING ASSOCIATIONS

This section is presently being compiled
and a comprehensive list will be available
for the next printing.

MY BEST PRACTICAL IDEA/TIP

How to "Keep Your Nurses & HealthCare Professionals for Life"

Name: _____ Date: _____

Position: _____ Dept.: _____

Dear Reader: "Keep Your Nurses For Life"

Here is my best idea/tip/suggestion on how to do a better job of reducing nurse turnover and improving retention:

_____

_____

_____

_____

_____

_____

_____

_____

_____

_____

_____

Permission to Publisher

❐ Yes   ❐ No

I give permission to publish my suggestions in "Keep Your Nurses & HealthCare Professionals For Life"

Signature _____

Home Mailing Address: _____

City: _____   State/Prov: _____

Zip/Postal: _____

Business Phone: (____)_____

Home Phone: (_____)_____

Forward to: Brian Lee CSP
Fax: 403-228-6776
or Email: brian@customlearning.com

E-LEARNING SEMINARS

Now available as an e-Seminar.

Also Available:

❏ Satisfaction Guaranteed
   How to Create Lifetime Customer Loyalty.

❏ The Genius of People Empowerment
   How to Motivate and Empower for Peak Performance

For Further Information Contact

       Bruce Lee

       1-800-667-7325

       bruce@customlearning.com

FEATURES OF E-SEMINARS

Full motion video-on-demand delivered through the Internet
- Experience an innovative new learning format using the best digital technology.

Slide show
- Follow the text presentation summarizing the main points, located next to the video screen.

Workbook
- Print out the Workbook before beginning the e-Seminar.
- Complete exercises, follow the diagrams, and take notes.
- Future reference document.

Frequently Asked Questions (FAQs) database
- Most frequently asked questions from e-Seminar participants, with answers from Brian Lee.

E-mail a Question
- Pause the video at anytime to e-mail questions to Brian Lee.

e-Bulletin
- Receive regular updates on e-Seminar content.

Pre-Assessment
- Evaluate your knowledge base. Take the Pre-Assessment before beginning the e-Seminar series.

Post-Assessment
- Measure what you have learned. Take the Post-Assessment after finishing the e-Seminar series.

Certificate of Completion
- Receive a Certificate upon completing all modules of the e-Seminar series.

BENEFITS OF E-SEMINARS

Valuable information
- Learn timely, topical, relevant and credible information presented by Brian Lee.
- Apply new skills to improve performance.
- Provides for ongoing professional development.
- Supports individual career advancement.

Learn at your time, your place, your pace
- Access on-demand e-Seminars anytime, anyplace, without time or geographical constraints.
- Learn at your own pace by pausing or replaying e-Seminars.

Save Time and Money
- Eliminate travel expenses and travel requirements.
- Reduce lost productivity due to convenient, flexible scheduling.
- Eliminate lost opportunity cost.
- Get the information when you need it.

E-SEMINAR BENEFITS FOR EMPLOYERS

Easy Accessibility

- Can be accessed from any geographical location that has a computer and Internet connection
- Available at any time of the day or week, regardless of time zones
- Scalable in that any number of employees can be assigned access
- Employees can access learning through the company's customized corporate education portal

Save Time

- No lost travel time getting to a seminar/workshop location
- No lost productivity time due to being away from workplace
- Schedule employees' learning experience at the company's convenience

Save Money

- No travel, accommodation, meal or meeting facility costs (for employees and trainers)
- Lost opportunity costs eliminated by accessing the learning when it is required
- Customized automated electronic billing or payment arrangements

Build Employee Knowledge and Increase Productivity

- Relevant, credible and highly usable business content provided by top experts in their field
- Instructional design features ensure effective knowledge transfer

- Same trainer and content ensures standardized and consistent company-wide training
- Individual users can learn privately and at their own pace for effective learning
- e-Seminar modular format allows numerous options for individualized learning requirements
- Ongoing coaching and mentoring available

Measure Results
- Customized reporting indicates when individual users accessed e-Seminars
- Pre-assessment identifies knowledge gaps or level of proficiency
- Post-testing measures effectiveness of transfer of knowledge
- Customized tracking of learning retention

READER SATISFACTION SURVEY

Brian Lee CSP
Author, Satisfaction Guaranteed

Dear Customer Satisfaction Professional:

This book came about as the result of years of experience com - bined with suggestions and ideas from hundreds of sources.

Feedback is truly the "breakfast of champions," and your expe - rience, ideas and suggestions will contribute to making this book better for future users.

Accordingly, I would appreciate it if you would share with me your observations by completing the attached Reader Satisfaction Survey.

With thanks in advance,

Brian C. Lee CSP

Reader Satisfaction Survey

To: Brian Lee CSP
Custom Learning Systems Group Ltd.
#200, 2133 Kensington Road N.W.
Calgary, Alberta Canada T2N 3R8
Fax: (403) 228-6776   Email: info@customlearning.com
Web site: www.keepyournursesforlife.com

From: Name:_____

Address:_____

City:_____

Province/State: _____ P.C./Zip:_____

Bus. Phone: (___)_____ Fax: (___)_____

Email:_____

Re: Comments/Observations – **Keep Your Nurses & Health Care Professionals For Life**

1. The best idea/technique gained and used from the book is:

_____

_____

_____

2. Comments, feedback received from Customer or others who have benefited from this book:

_____

_____

_____

3. Suggestions for improving existing ideas, content, format:

_____

_____

4. Suggested "Best Idea" that could be added:

    _____

    _____

    _____

5. I became aware of the book by/through:

    _____

    _____

    _____

6. P.S.

    _____

    _____

    _____

    _____

7. On a scale of 1 – 5, **Keep Your Nurses & HealthCare Professionals For Life** was:

    (5 = Valuable, 1 = Poor)

1.	Practical, helpful and relevant	5	4	3	2	1
2.	Well-organized	5	4	3	2	1
3.	Easy to use, reader friendly	5	4	3	2	1
4.	Good value for the money	5	4	3	2	1
5.	Overall I rate **Keep Your Nurses & HealthCare Professionals For Life**	5	4	3	2	1

    6. What could we do to serve you better?

    _____

    _____

    _____

    _____

    _____

Brian Lee CSP Presents...
Keep Your Nurses & HealthCare Professionals For Life

"The 4 Imperatives of How to Inspire, Retain, Motivate and Empower, Patient Focussed Nurses (& Everybody Else)"

4 Volume CD Set (PCD3536)
Regular $169.00

Special Price of $125⁰⁰

Keep Your Nurses For Life CD Set ___ copies @ $125.00 = $_____

Keep Your Nurses For Life Book ___ copies @ $ 29.95 = $_____

Postage & Handling ___ items @ $ 7.50 = $_____

G.S.T. $_____

Total $_____

Ship To:

Name: _____ Title: _____

Organization: _____

Address: _____

City: _____ State/Prov.: _____

Country: _____ Zip/P.C.: _____

Daytime Phone: _____ Fax: _____

Email: _____

Method of Payment

Credit Card orders can be faxed or phoned in.

☐ Cheque #

Made payable to:

Custom Learning Systems Group Ltd.
#200, 2133 Kensington Road N.W..
Calgary, Alberta T2N 3R8
Fax: (403) 228-6776
Toll Free: 1-800-667-7325

☐ Charge to:
☐ MasterCard ☐ Visa

Card #:

_____

Expiry: _____

Cardholder
Signature:

_____

Order Form

Ordered by:

Name:_____ Title: _____
Organization: _____
Address: _____
City:_____ State/Prov.:_____
Country:_____ Zip/P.C.: _____
Daytime Phone:_____ Fax: _____
Email: _____

Ship to: (if different from above)

Name:_____ Title: _____
Organization: _____
Address: _____
City: _____ State/Prov.:_____
Country:_____ Zip/P.C.: _____
Daytime Phone:_____ Fax: _____

Order:

Qty	Title	Order Number	Audio	Video	Other	Unit Price	Total

Shipping & Handling

$ 0 – $ 50	$ 8.95	$151 – $200	$11.95
$ 51 – $100	$ 9.95	$201 – $250	$12.95
$101 – $150	$10.95	$251 – $300	$13.95

For orders totalling over $300, add $1 for each additional $50 of purchases.

Merchandise Total	
Shipping & Handling	
Sub-Total	
G.S.T.	
GRAND TOTAL	

Method of Payment

Credit Card orders can be faxed or phoned in.

☐ Cheque #
Made payable to:

Custom Learning Systems Group Ltd.
#200, 2133 Kensington Road N.W..
Calgary, Alberta T2N 3R8
Fax: (403) 228-6776
Toll Free: 1-800-667-7325

☐ Charge to:
  ☐ MasterCard   ☐ Visa
Card #:
_____
Expiry: _____
Cardholder
Signature:

6 Powerful Reasons to Put Brian Lee to Work for You:

1. **Brian Lee is a World-Class Author:**
   In addition to his busy speaking calendar, Brian brings the credibility of having authored four books:

   - **Satisfaction Guaranteed**
     How to Satisfy Every Customer Every Time

   - **Leadership Strategies**
     A Leadership Anthology with introduction by F. Lee Bailey

   - **One Minute Name Memory**
     How to Remember Every Name – Every Time – Forever!

   - **The Wedding MC**
     How to MC and Speak at Weddings

   Brian also has produced two dozen popular audio and video cassette albums, as well as numerous articles.

2. **Brian Lee Gets Immediate Results:**
   With a track record of personally speaking to over 750,000 people in the past 14 years as a professional speaker, Brian consistently earns an astonishing audience rating of 4.8 (out of a possible 5). Each year, Brian receives hundreds of letters testifying to the long-term impact and influence he has in the work place and with people's careers.

3. **Brian Lee's Remarkable Customizing Skills are his Trademark:**

   Every speaking engagement is created from scratch for each new audience.

   The quote from Rick Martinez's unsolicited letter (right) is typical of the feedback received from literally hundreds of meeting planners who consistently rave about Brian's unique 37 step process of custom-tailoring and personalizing each and every presentation, right down to the detail of remembering the names of everyone in his audience.

4. **Brian Lee Educates, Empowers, Entertains and Recommends:**

   Brian is not just a motivational speaker. He is a leading-edge, high content educator who enhances his crystal clear delivery skills with a unique combination of sincerity, relevant humour and passion, with step-by-step recommendations for implementation. Put Brian on the platform for you, then get ready to see your people take action.

5. **Brian Lee is a CSP – Certified Speaking Professional**

   Certified Speaking Professional (CSP) is an earned designation conferred by the National Speakers Association to recognize demonstrated commitment to the speaking profession through proven speaking experience. In 1993, Brian Lee received this prestigious certification. One of less than 20 speakers in Canada and less than 500 people in the world have passed the rigorous criteria to attain this coveted designation.

6. **Brian Lee IS Canada's "Mr. Enthusiasm"**

   Brian Lee focuses on the joy that is gained from a job well done. The nickname "Mr. Enthusiasm" wasn't created by a public relations firm, but rather "leapt" from the pages of tens of thousands of audience evaluation forms from Brian's diary of over 2,500 speaking engagements during the past 14 years.

Ⓦ **Westinghouse Hanford Company**

"I am especially impressed with your ability to grasp the issues we're struggling with at Westinghouse in the nuclear industry and to be able to incorporate them into the seminars. In fact, one Human Resource manager commented, 'I'm embarrassed because Brian knows more about my company than I do.' Your research and homework obviously paid off."

Rick Martinez,
Human Resources Specialist
Westinghouse Hanford Company

BRIAN LEE CSP – KEYNOTE/SEMINAR TOPICS

Yes, we may be interested in a Brian Lee CSP presentation on:

A   The following topic(s) that are listed in the
audio/video/book library listed on pages 117 to 125:

Title(s)_____

_____

B   The following topic(s) listed below:

❏ Feature Conference Keynotes
  ❏ Thriving on Change
  ❏ Anything You Can Do,
    You Can Do Better
  ❏ The Six Secrets of
    People Empowerment
  ❏ The Challenge of
    Leadership Excellence
  ❏ The Six Secrets of
    Personal Enthusiasm
  ❏ Reinventing Training
  ❏ Succeed From Adversity
  ❏ Creating Opportunity
    Through Personal
    Entrepreneurship

❏ Customer Satisfaction
  ❏ The 13 Secrets of Creating
    World-Class Customer
    Satisfaction
  ❏ Change Your Culture or Be
    Doomed to Repeat the Past

❏ Health Care
  ❏ The Service Excellence
    Advisor Train the Trainer
    Initiative
  ❏ The Challenge of
    Sustaining and Growing a
    Medical Practice Through
    the Year 2000
  ❏ Growing Through Cultural
    Diversity

❏ Team Work
  ❏ Building Self-Empowered
    Teams
  ❏ Creating High Performance
    Teamwork with People You
    Don't Know or Like

❏ Change Leadership
  ❏ Take Charge of our Future
    Change Leadership Summit

❏ Communication
  ❏ Communication Dynamics
  ❏ Why People Do What They Do

❏ Professional Development
  ❏ The Dynamics of Effective
    Boards
  ❏ The Power of Professional
    Development
  ❏ G.O.A.L. Master

❏ Government
  ❏ Vision, Values and
    Empowering Public Sector
    Leadership
  ❏ S.E.R.V.I.C.E. Your
    Constituents and Save
    Your Sanity
  ❏ The Wit and Humour of
    Politics

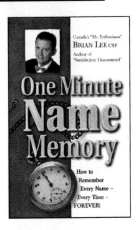

Satisfaction Guaranteed
by Brian Lee CSP
*"Master the Six Secrets of
Creating World-Class Customer
Satisfaction"*
(PB600) **$19.95/29.95**

One Minute Name Memory
by Brian Lee CSP
*"How to Remember Every
Name – Every Time – Forever!"*
(PB1455C) **$24.95**

Wisdom Worth Quoting
by Brian Lee CSP
*"52 Certificates Suitable
for Framing"*
(PB200) **$39.95**

The Wedding M.C.
by Brian Lee CSP
*"How to M.C. and Speak at
Weddings. A step-by-step
guide."*
(PB400) **$29.95**

Advanced Presentation Skills
Train the Trainer Course by Brian Lee CSP
"How to Design & Deliver the Best Training Program of your Life Every Time"

12-Volume Audio Album
(PA2501) **$177.77**

Also Available:
Six-Volume Video Album
(PV2501) **$195.00**

Advanced Presentation Skills (APS) Participant Workbook
by Brian Lee CSP
A 250-page manual to accompany the APS 12-hour course (above).
Learning Guide (W2501) **$95.00**

Special Offer — **10% Off when you buy the whole set!**

The Presentation Skills "MASTER LIBRARY"

APS 12-Audio Set	PA2501	$177.77
APS Learning Guide	W2501	$ 95.00
One Minute Name Memory 2-Audio Set	PA1455C	$ 24.95
Audience Participation Video	PV2555	$ 95.00
The Wedding M.C. Book	PB400	$ 29.95
Total		$ 422.67

All 5 products **$379**

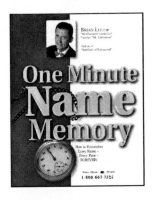

The Six Secrets of
One Minute Name Memory
by Brian Lee CSP
"How to Remember Every Name –
Every Time – Forever!"

Two-Volume Audio Album
(PA1455C) **$24.95**

Also Available:
One-Video (PV1455C) **$95.00**
Book (PB1455C) **$24.95**

The Genius of Great
Audience Participation
by Brian Lee CSP
"How to Empower and Create
Audience Ownership"

One-Volume Video Album
(PV2555) **$95.00**

The Wedding M.C.
by Brian Lee CSP
"How to M.C. and Speak at
Weddings. A step-by-step guide."
Book (PB400) **$29.95**

Six Star™ Customer Satisfaction Series
by Brian Lee CSP
"Creating World-Class Customer Satisfaction"

12-Volume Audio Album
(PA544A) **$177.77**

6-Volume Video Album
(PV544A) **$595.00**

Individual Six Star Customer Satisfaction Albums

❏ **Satisfaction Guaranteed**
"How to Create Lifetime Customer Loyalty"
2-Video Set (PV545A) $175.00
2-Audio Set (PA545A) $29.95
16 pg. Workbook (W545A) $3.00
130 pg. Book (PB600) $19.95

❏ **Winning With Difficult Customers**
"How You Can Say to the Most Difficult Customer in the World – Come and Get Me!"
2-Video Set (PV550A) $175.00
2-Audio Set (PA550A) $29.95
16 pg. Workbook (W550A) $3.00

❏ **Stress-Free Service Excellence**
"How to Create a Stress-Free Environment for You and Your Customers"
2-Video Set (PV555A) $175.00
2-Audio Set (PA555A) $29.95
16 pg. Workbook (W555A) $3.00

❏ **One Minute Service Selling**
"How to Gain a Competitive Advantage by Helping Others Get What they Want"
2-Video Set (PV560A) $175.00
2-Audio Set (PA560A) $29.95
16 pg. Workbook (W560A) $3.00

❏ **Managing Moments of Truth**
"How to Continuously Improve Customer Satisfaction"
2-Video Set (PV565A) $175.00
2-Audio Set (PA565A) $29.95
16 pg. Workbook (W565A) $3.00

❏ **Self Esteem & Service Superstars**
"Enhanced Self-Esteem Equals Enhanced Service Excellence"
2-Video Set (PV570A) $175.00
2-Audio Set (PA570A) $29.95
16 pg. Workbook (W570A) $3.00

Service Empowerment Leadership Course
by Brian Lee CSP
"Creating a Customer-Driven Culture through People Empowerment and Continuous Improvement"

12-Volume Audio Album
(PA2320A) **$177.77**

6-Volume Video Album
(PV2320A) **$595.00**

Individual Service Empowerment Leadership Course Albums

☐ **Vision, Values & Inspired Leadership**
"How to Create a Customer-Driven Culture"
2-Video Set (PV2340A) $175.00
2-Audio Set (PA2340A) $29.95
16 pg. Workbook (W2340A) $3.00

☐ **Thriving on Change**
"How to Survive and Thrive in the Midst of Change"
2-Video Set (PV2345A) $175.00
2-Audio Set (PA2345A) $29.95
16 pg. Workbook (W2345A) $3.00

☐ **The Genius of People Empowerment**
"How to Motivate and Empower for Peak Performance"
2-Video Set (PV2350A) $175.00
2-Audio Set (PA2350A) $29.95
16 pg. Workbook (W2350A) $3.00

☐ **The Power of Continuous Improvement**
"How to Measure and Significantly Improve Customer Perception and Satisfaction"
2-Video Set (PV2355A) $175.00
2-Audio Set (PA2355A) $29.95
16 pg. Workbook (W2355A) $3.00

☐ **Total Quality Leadership**
"How to Implement the 13 Steps of Total Quality Process Improvement"
2-Video Set (PV2360A) $175.00
2-Audio Set (PA2360A) $29.95
16 pg. Workbook (W2360A) $3.00

☐ **The Challenge of Innovative Excellence**
"How to Continuously Improve Service While Creatively Reducing Costs"
2-Video Set (PV2365A) $175.00
2-Audio Set (PA2365A) $29.95
16 pg. Workbook (W2365A) $3.00

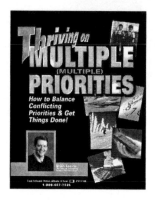

Thriving on Multiple (Multiple) Priorities
by Brian Lee CSP
"How to Balance Conflicting Priorities & Get Things Done"

Two-Volume Video Album
(PV1786) **$175.00**

Four-Volume Audio Album
(PA1782) **$69.95**

The 7 Attributes of Meeting Mastery
by Brian Lee CSP
"How to Organize the Best Meeting of Your Life Every time"

Four-Volume Audio Album
(PA2742A) **$69.95**

Stress Master
by Brian Lee CSP
"How to Survive and Thrive in Spite of Stress & Fatigue"

Six-Volume Audio Album
(PA1776) **$89.95**

Winning with Difficult People
by Brian Lee CSP
"How You Can Say to the Most Difficult People in the World... Come and Get Me"

Two-Volume Video Album
(PV1793) **$195.00**

Six-Volume Audio Album
(PA1793) **$89.95**

The 13 Secrets of Creating World-Class Customer Satisfaction
by Brian Lee CSP
"How to Create a Customer-Driven Culture Through People Empowerment & Continuous Improvement"

One-Volume Video Album
(PV481) **$95.95**

Anything You Can Do... You Can Do Better
by Brian Lee CSP
"How to Put the Power of Excellence to Work in Your Professional Career & Personal Life"

Two-Volume Audio Album
(PA408E) **$24.95**

www.keepyournursesforlife.com

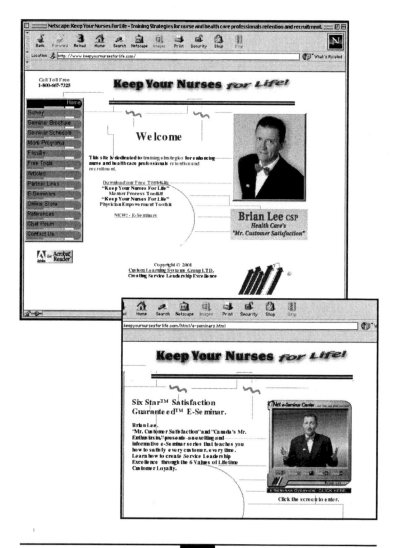